"Jeff Arthurs clearly and thoroughly shows how the parts of narrative—plot, character, setting, and point of view—combine to bring biblical stories to life. He then goes on to show how your sermon can use the same narrative skills to capture your twenty-first century listeners. Continuous biblical and sermon examples make this a book preachers will file and return to when preparing messages on passages he mentions."

> – Don Sunukjian, Professor of Preaching Emeritus, Talbot School of Theology

"Jeffrey D. Arthurs is one of the best narrative preachers I know. As a gifted exegete, homiletician, and storyteller, I am grateful that he has gifted preachers, pulpits, and people in the pews with his latest, *How to Preach Narrative*. Arthurs showcases the beauty of the narrative genre in Scripture and provides experience-proven techniques for telling the story of God in God's way. Pick up a copy today. Your listeners will thank you for it. They may even respond with a story of their own."

> – Matthew D. Kim, Professor of Practical Theology and Raborn Chair of Pastoral Leadership, Truett Theological Seminary, Baylor University

"This book is a wonderful combination of the theoretical foundations and the practical applications involved in preaching narrative texts. Jeff knows the beautiful struggle of preaching and with this book he makes the struggle easier for all of us, mentoring us in the joy and craft of preaching. I strongly recommend it for book groups, classes, and anyone who wants to give their preaching some new life."

> – Mary Hulst, University Pastor, Calvin University

T0376354

How to Preach Narrative

*For my friends and cruise-mates:*
*David and Sharon, JD and Kim*
*And my wife, Liz*

*Your lives are incarnated narrative sermons to me.*

# HOW TO PREACH NARRATIVE

❈

JEFFREY D. ARTHURS

Fontes

# Contents

# Series Introduction

The Bible is the best-selling book of all time. There are various reasons for that—it feeds us spiritually; gives us hope; points us to the Triune God; and shows us where we came from and where we are going. There's another reason: the Bible is great literature; just plain great. Captivating narratives, wry proverbs, dark prophecies, catalogues of laws, and practical but theologically deep epistles populate its pages.

However, the literary nature of the Bible creates a problem for preaching. What's a preacher to do with that fact that the Bible is literature? Are we supposed to create sermonic-poems when we preach psalms? Are we supposed to leave our meaning opaque when we preach certain parables? If the text is a story must the sermon be a story? What's a preacher to do?

One thing preachers could do, and have done, is to ignore the fact that the Bible is literature. Turn a deaf ear and blind eye to its literary qualities. Feed each text into the homiletical mill and crank out sermon after sermon as uniform as hotdogs. The authors of this series reject that option. Our conviction is that God inspired not only the content of the Bible, but also its forms. Cranking out homiletical hotdogs from quirky parables, awe-inspiring miracle stories, kaleidoscopic visions, and emotive lyric poetry violates authorial intention. Ronald Allen famously quipped: "To change the form of preaching to a form not clearly representative of the text is akin to covering the cathedral at Chartres with vinyl siding."[1]

---

1 Ronald J. Allen, "Shaping Sermons by the Language of the Text," in *Preaching Biblically,* ed. Don M. Wardlaw (Westminster, 1983), 30.

The authors share another conviction: preaching should be interesting. Holding an audience's attention is largely a matter of content—showing how the ancient Word applies to today's needs and interests—but it is also a matter of form. A steady diet of hotdogs is unappetizing.

So, how can preachers be biblical in form as well as content? That question is the impetus of this series called *Preaching Biblical Literature.* In trim and readable volumes, the reader will encounter methods and strategies for preaching the various genres of the Bible. We want to give preachers recipes for sermons that are as varied as the literature in the Bible itself.

Our goal is to provide succinct descriptions of these literary forms with concrete suggestions for preaching in genre-sensitive ways. Each volume is grounded in biblical and literary scholarship and applies those disciplines to homiletics. With plenty of examples in each chapter, as well as sample sermons at the end of each book, our hope is to teach and model how to preach biblical literature biblically. Here's to stamping out hotdogs. Let's get cooking.

Jeffrey D. Arthurs
Kenneth J. Langley

# Introduction

*Anyone who loves the Bible must value the story, for whatever else the Bible is, it is a book of stories.*[1]

– Haddon Robinson

EVERYONE LOVES A STORY, but not everyone loves a sermon based on a story. Why is that? Maybe because sermons often desiccate the Bible's narratives. This book and the others in the *Preaching Biblical Literature* series help us avoid preaching sermons as dry as last year's bird nest. Let us avoid Ralph Waldo Emerson's description of his own lectures: "fine things, pretty things, wise things, but no arrows, no axes, no nectar, no growling, no transpiercing, no loving, no enchantment."[2]

The preacher's inclination to desiccate is unfortunate when we consider that we live in a story-saturated culture. In fact, it may not be an overstatement to say that stories pervade *all* cultures across time. Today story is going strong in film, novels, magazines, and podcasts; and in the United States old radio shows like Paul Harvey's "The Rest of the Story," and more recent shows like Garrison Keillor's "A Prairie Home Companion," not to mention hundreds of podcasts such as "This American Life," testify to our ubiquitous love of a good story.

---

1 Haddon W. Robinson, *Biblical Preaching: The Development and Delivery of Expository Messages*, 3rd ed. (Baker, 2014), 90.

2 Ralph Waldo Emerson, *The Journals and Miscellaneous Notebooks of Ralph Waldo Emerson*, 7:339; quoted in *The Cambridge Companion to Ralph Waldo Emerson*, ed. Joel Porte and Saundra Morris (Cambridge University Press, 1999), 79.

Philosopher Stephen Crites argues that story may have universal appeal because we perceive life itself as a story: people (characters) perform actions (plot) in space and time (setting). Crites writes, "The formal quality of experience through time is inherently narrative," and, "Stories give qualitative substance to the form of experience because [experience] is itself an incipient story."[3] Similarly, New Testament scholar N. T. Wright talks about the "storied and relational nature of human consciousness."[4] Our minds seem predisposed to see the kaleidoscopic events of life not as "a tale told by an idiot" (*Macbeth*), but as a plot that progresses purposefully through conflict, complication, and resolution. Writing about the appeal of narrative, Jonathan Gottschall makes the bold claim that the "human mind was shaped *for* story, so that it could be shaped *by* story."[5]

Because story is universal, we are not surprised that it is the largest genre in the Bible. More than half of God's Word is narrative—Genesis, Judges, Ruth, 1 and 2 Samuel, Esther, Luke, and so forth. Other books are generic hybrids as when Job combines wisdom and narrative, and Acts weaves numerous speeches into the structure of a travelogue. Many parables are stories, and narrative sections punctuate the prophets.[6] The Bible's preference for narrative resides in theology as well as epistemology (how we think). That is, the Bible presents God as active and purposeful, guiding the works of his hands from creation through the fall into redemption and consummation. He is the director of a play that has a beginning, middle, and end.

Like all genres and portions of Scripture, the narratives of the Bible teach us about God and humanity, but this genre tends to be indirect, "showing" more than "telling." I'll return to the distinction

---

3 Stephen Crites, "The Narrative Quality of Experience," *Journal of the American Academy of Religion* 29 (September 1971): 291, 297.

4 N. T. Wright, *The New Testament and the People of God* (Fortress, 1992), 61.

5 Jonathan Gottschall, *The Storytelling Animal: How Stories Make Us Human* (Mariner Books/Houghton Mifflin Harcourt, 2013), 56.

6 To the extent that a parable is a narrative (such as the Good Samaritan), or a generic hybrid contains narratives (such as the Gospels and some of the prophets), this book will apply to those genres as well. But the special provenance of this book is historical narrative. I define the genre in Chapter 1.

between "showing" and "telling" in the chapters that follow, but my point here is that narrative communicates with its own set of formal devices, and the set can make interpretation a challenge. As the *Westminster Confession* observes, "All things in Scripture are not alike plain in themselves" (1.7).

So, we need an approach to interpretation that is conversant with the tools of narrative—plot, character, setting, and point of view. Those four features of the genre will be the backbone of Part One of this book as we take a literary-rhetorical approach to exegesis. Each feature will receive its own chapter as we ask not only *what* authors communicate, but also *how* they communicate. We are concerned with form as well as content. I hold a conservative view of Scripture, believing that the form of the text along with its content are both matters of authorial intention. Form is not simply the wrapper around the sweet—an indigestible barrier to be discarded as we scramble to reach the dainty. It is more like the music that accompanies the lyrics of a song. Form is the author's strategy to prompt a response to the content.

Standard issues of exegesis such as theology, context, word study, grammar, history, and culture are perfectly compatible with the special provenance of this book: literary-rhetorical analysis. With Robert Alter, I contend that "we shall come much closer to the range of intended meanings—theological, psychological, moral, or whatever—of the biblical tale by understanding precisely how it is told."[7] This book asks the question that John Ciardi has asked of another genre: *how* does a narrative mean?[8]

Part Two of this book shifts from exegesis to homiletics, suggesting how to preach narrative in a genre-sensitive way, not only saying what the text says, but also doing what the text does. That is the key—doing what the text does—reproducing the effects the author intended: the attention-holding power of plot, the emotionally-gripping appeal of character, and the imagination-stirring descriptions of setting. I do not argue that preachers must slavishly copy the form of the text; but I do contend that the form of narrative is easily assimilated into the form of the sermon and should be

---

7 Robert Alter, *The Art of Biblical Narrative* (Basic Books, 1981), 179.
8 John Ciardi, *How Does a Poem Mean?* 2nd ed. (Houghton Mifflin, 1975).

our default choice when preaching from narrative. Chapters 6 to 10 will offer a basketful of strategies to do what the text does.

But I'm getting ahead of myself. We need to start at the very beginning (a very good place to start). Part One helps us prepare for preaching narrative. Chapter 1 will define narrative. Then we will be set for a deep dive into the literary-rhetorical features of the genre: plot, character, setting, and point of view (Chapters 2–5).

## For Further Study

- Long, Thomas. *Preaching and the Literary Forms of the Bible*. Fortress, 1989.
- Ryken, Leland. *Words of Delight*. Baker, 1992.
- Ryken, Leland. "The Bible as Literature and Expository Preaching." Pages 38–53 in *Preach the Word*. Edited by Leland Ryken and Todd Wilson. Crossway, 2007.

### Talk about It

Have you heard a sermon from narrative that reproduced the effects of the genre? Who preached it? Describe it. Conversely, have you heard a sermon from narrative that sucked the life out of the story?

### Dig Deeper

Reflect on the claim that expository preachers pay attention to form as well as content. Do you agree? Would you qualify the statement?

### Practice

Listen to a classic sermon from narrative, R. G. Lee's "Payday Someday" (easily found with an internet search). First preached in 1919, and subsequently preached more than 1000 times before Dr. Lee died in 1978, the language of this sermon is from another era and may strike your ear as quaint or dated, but see if you would consider it an example of "genre-sensitive" preaching.

Part One

# Biblical Narrative as Literature and Rhetoric

1

# Defining Biblical Narrative

*Without knowledge of literature pure the-*
*ology cannot at all endure... . Certainly it*
*is my desire that there shall be as many*
*poets and rhetoricians as possible, because*
*I see that by these studies, as by no other*
*means, people are wonderfully fitted for*
*the grasping of sacred truth and for han-*
*dling it skillfully and happily.*[1]

Martin Luther

IN THIS CHAPTER we will survey the contours of narrative from a high altitude, and then we will be ready to descend into the details of the genre in Chapters 2–5.

The narratives of the Bible tend to use story more than proposition as a way of interpreting the world. For example, the narratives would probably convey the idea "God is love" as "God so loved the world that he... ." Unfortunately, we have been taught that stories belong in the nursery with a picture book or on the beach with a paperback novel, but when it comes to ideas, adults can take the medicine without sugar coating. Yet, the low performance review we file for narrative is not in keeping with the fact that God has chosen to communicate his written word primarily as story. So, this chapter aims at expanding our education.

Starting from a high altitude, let me offer a definition of biblical

---

1 Quoted in David J. A. Clines, "Story and Poem: The Old Testament as Literature and as Scripture," *Interpretation* 34 (April 1980): 115.

narrative: *a historically accurate, artistically and rhetorically sophisticated, theologically saturated account of characters and events in a setting, intended to be analyzed and applied for edification.* I will unpack this definition in five sections giving expanded development to a few of the sections.

## Historically Accurate

I hold a conservative doctrine of Scripture. I believe that the events narrated happened, even the miracles. Of course, in reducing the events to writing, the authors of the Bible necessarily selected and shaped their material—the world could not contain the books if *everything* were recorded—but what is recorded is historically accurate. This does not deny an author's artistic handlings of material and rhetorical purpose; it only affirms that what is recorded is truthful.

This view of biblical narrative as history is congruent with the rhetorical aims of the authors. As Rhoads, Dewey, and Michie say of the book of Mark: "The rhetoric of Mark's narrative is compelling in large part because the reader understands it to be based on real events. The power of Mark's narrative was rooted in the conviction that the rule of God had actually arrived, that the anointed messiah had come, been killed, and been raised."[2] Christianity is rare, if not unique, among the religions of the world in emphasizing history, working from the conviction that God works in and with the doings of individuals and nations; and without the incarnation—God invading the planet bodily in the person of Jesus—there would be no Christianity.

## Artistically Sophisticated

Have no doubts about it: the narratives of the Bible are works of art. This does not contradict the point above because "artistic" need not connote "fiction." Rather, the genre of historical narrative is well able to display the marks of literary art such as beauty,

---

2 David Rhoads, Joanna Dewey, and Donald Michie, *Mark as Story: An Introduction to the Narrative of a* Gospel, 2nd ed. (Fortress, 1999), 144.

universality of theme, seriousness of subject matter, excellence of form, heightened affect, masterful language, and the ability to do justice to the complexity of life. With Robert Alter, author of the groundbreaking *The Art of Biblical Narrative*, I see a "complete interfusion of literary art with theological, moral, or historiosophical vision."[3] Meir Sternberg makes the same case in his magisterial *The Poetics of Biblical Narrative* as he describes the genre's interplay of ideological, historical, and aesthetic impulses.[4] Each of these impulses could easily shove the others aside, or as Sternberg puts it, if given free rein each "would pull in a different direction and either win the tug of war or tear the work apart."[5] Ideology tends to be prescriptive and blunt, not indirect and artistic; historiography tends to state only facts, as plain as an encyclopedia or cookbook; and the aesthetic impulse wants primarily to revel in imagination to create an experience. Yet in biblical narrative the impulses sing in harmony.

As I rhapsodize about the artistry of biblical narrative, let me not overstate my case. The artistry of the genre can be ranged on a sliding scale. The book of Ruth is high art on a par with the psalms with its wordplay, symbolism, plot development, and characterization; but the genealogies of Chronicles are much more mundane. In fact, they may not even "deserve" to be called "narrative" as they employ a different set of techniques to carry out their purposes. The genre of genealogy employs plot, character, and setting only on a rudimentary level.

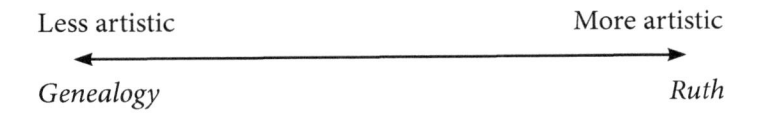

Less artistic           More artistic

*Genealogy*           *Ruth*

*Figure 1.1: Biblical Narrative as Art, a Sliding Scale*

---

3 Robert Alter, *The Art of Biblical Narrative* (Basic Books, 1981), 19.

4 Meir Sternberg, *The Poetics of Biblical Narrative: Ideological Reading and the Drama of Reading* (Indiana University Press, 1985), 41. Thomas G. Long reflects on Sternberg's argument in *Preaching and the Literary Forms of the Bible* (Fortress, 1989), 67–70.

5 Sternberg, *The Poetics of Biblical Narrative*, 41–44.

As an ancient art form with theological and ethical designs, we must judge biblical narrative on its own terms, not simply by the canons of modern literature. For example, modern narrative luxuriates in detailed description, but one of the most noticeable features of biblical narrative (and nearly all ancient narrative) is brevity and terseness. This genre is *laconic*, rarely embellishing or using explicit commentary. The narratives of the Bible are not like the stories of John Grisham or the histories of David McCullough with their extended descriptions, and this may give us the idea that the Bible is primitive, like children's literature. Yet the genre carries a freight of meaning out of proportion to the size of its packaging. Erich Auerbach made this case brilliantly in the first chapter of *Mimesis*. Auerbach compares Genesis to Homer's *Odyssey* demonstrating that the laconic quality of biblical narrative is a technique of profound art, not primitiveness.[6]

An example of skillful brevity is the repetition of the word "send" (Heb. *shalah*) in 2 Samuel 10–12.[7] In those three chapters the term appears twenty-three times, and in the larger context of chapters 9–20 it is used forty-four times. In the rest of the book it appears only thirteen times. King David does most of the sending: he *sends* for Bathsheba, *sends* for Uriah, *sends* Uriah back to battle, and so forth. The author shows us David's regal power as he sends people hither and thither to do his will, but it is regal power debased. David flouts God's will and abuses the people even though his power was a gift bestowed on a "nobody." Eventually God *sends* Nathan the prophet (12:1) to end the ironic tragedy of David's little exercise of power. The author tersely shows us that godly rulers should use their power in godly ways.

Whereas biblical narrative's laconic style differs from modern storytelling, it shares another feature—the ubiquitous tendency to "show" rather than "tell." For instance, to convey the idea that God is sovereign, the author of Esther shows what appear to be coincidences, seemingly random events, in the administration of the palace. Donald Sunukjian uses the analogy of a large doll's house.

6  Erich Auerbach, *Mimesis: The Representation of Reality in Western Literature*, trans. Willard Trask (Princeton University Press, 1953), 3–23.

7  See Abraham Kuruvilla, *Privilege the Text: A Theological Hermeneutic for Preaching* (Moody, 2013), 120–121.

The owner of the house reaches in to arrange furniture, figures, and events. The hand of the owner may or may not be seen; nevertheless, the hand disposes everything.[8] God arranges the furniture of the book of Ruth similarly. Ruth and Naomi serendipitously returned to Bethlehem at the beginning of barley harvest (1:22). Wasn't that lucky? Ruth "happened to come of the part of the field belonging to Boaz" (2:3). More luck! Then, "Behold, the redeemer of whom Boaz had spoken" (4:1) happened to come by at the right time, and this enabled Boaz to redeem Ruth. What lucky timing! No, the author is not showing us luck. He is showing the hand of God arranging the times and seasons of individuals and nations.

Examples of "showing" are present on every page of biblical narrative. Thus, the process of exegeting the authorial intention regarding theology and ethics is similar to the way we reflect on film, novel, or song.[9] The descriptive question, "What happens in the story?" should lead to the interpretive question, "What is the author driving at?" As Ryken states, "At both levels, stories are at least a distant literary relative of the riddle, teasing us into a process of discovery."[10]

Of course, we must not exaggerate the point about showing and telling. Biblical narrative *does* sometimes punctuate the showing with propositions, as when the author comments on the David's abuse of power: "The thing that David had done displeased the Lord" (2 Sam 11:27). Discursive comments like this keep readers on the rails as they discern authorial intention.

The showing-style of biblical narrative allows for a complex handling of doctrine and ethics. Life is complicated and messy, to which the Bible's stories say "amen!" David is a man after God's own heart, but he also abuses power and unleashes a Pandora's box of family dysfunction. Thomas is a doubter, but he is also resolute, willing to follow Jesus unto death. Biblical characters rarely wear black hats and white. Instead, their hats shade between off-white

---

8 Don Sunukjian, "A Night in Persia," https://www.preachingtoday.com/sermons/sermons/2005/august/0364.html.

9 John Goldingay, "Biblical Narrative and Systematic Theology," in *Between Two Horizons: Spanning New Testament Studies and Systematic Theology*, ed. Joel B. Green and Max Turner (Eerdmans, 2000), 124.

10 Leland Ryken, *How to Read the Bible as Literature* (Zondervan, 1984), 58.

and dark-gray. Goldingay says that biblical characters are like the characters in film noir: everyone has his or her weaknesses and there are few unadulterated heroes.[11] This helps readers stay focused on God, the ultimate protagonist of narratives in the Bible, and as Goldingay observes, this helps us "leave church less sombered than we leave the cinema."[12]

Not only are characters complex, but situations are too. The book of Acts shows us two truths that may not seem to belong together: the gospel spreads with the irresistible force of a tsunami, but this happens simultaneously with persecution and rejection. Gaventa observes: "To eliminate either of them is to miss something essential to the Lukan story."[13]

## Rhetorically Sophisticated

Rhetoric is the art of persuasion. In the ancient world the term "rhetoric" was associated with oratory—speech making in the law courts, political assembly, and ceremonial occasions. Training in rhetoric was ubiquitous throughout the Greco-Roman world, and most of the Church Fathers were schooled in the art. In the Middle Ages and continuing to the present, the term has been broadened to include any form of communication that produces effects on a given audience.

The rhetorical nature of the Bible is widely acknowledged today, and rhetorical criticism has become a standard tool of exegesis.

| |
|---|
| • Bernard Ramm: "Holy Scripture is not a theoretical book of theological abstraction, but a book that intends to have a mighty influence on the lives of its readers." <br> *Protestant Biblical Interpretation*, 3rd edition (Baker, 1985), 113. |
| • John Sailhammer: "A text is … an embodiment of an author's intention, that is a strategy designed to carry out that intention." <br> *Introduction to Old Testament Theology* (Baker, 1995), 46–47. |

---

11  Goldingay, "Biblical Narrative and Systematic Theology," 136.

12  Ibid.

13  Beverly Roberts Gaventa, "Towards a Theology of Acts: Reading and Rereading," *Interpretation* 42 (1988): 157.

> - Erich Auerbach: "The world of Scripture is not satisfied with claiming to be a historically true reality—it insists that it is the only real world... . The Scripture stories do not ... court our favor, they do not flatter us... . They seek to subject us and if we refuse to be subjected, we are rebels."
>   *Mimesis: The Representation of Reality in Western Literature,* trans. Willard Trask (Princeton Univ. Press, 1953), 14–15.
> - Dale Patrick and Allen Scult: "The Bible's main form of exposition, the narrative, is most appropriately characterized as primary rhetoric, its ... objective being to persuade its audience."
>   *Rhetoric and Biblical Interpretation* (Almond, 1990), 29.
> - Meir Sternberg: Old Testament narrative is "a transaction between the narrator and the audience on whom [the narrator] wishes to produce a certain effect by way of certain strategies."
>   *The Poetics of Biblical Narrative: Ideological Literature and the Drama of Reading* (Indiana Univ. Press, 1985), 1.

*Figure 1.2: Rhetorical Nature of Biblical Narrative*

Chapters 2–5 will look closely at the set of tools narrative uses for persuasion (plot, character, setting, and point of view), and Part Two, Chapters 6–10, will suggest how we can do similar things in our sermons. But in this chapter, I simply wish to assert that the authors of the Bible consciously intended to influence their readers.

Rhetorical analysis is perfectly companionable with grammatical-historical exegesis. Rhetorical analysis unpacks one aspect of the author's intention: the target he aimed at and the techniques he used to take aim. For the expository preacher, such a perspective is invaluable as we seek to say what the text says and do what the text does. Wayne Booth's description of rhetorical criticism has relevance for preachers as well as storytellers: "Rhetorical study is the study of use, of purpose pursued, targets hit or missed, practices illuminated, not for the sake of pure knowledge, but of further (and improved) practice... . We want to know *why* one story or technique works better than another, because ... our practices as tellers and listeners can always be improved."[14]

One way narrative rhetoric works is by being concrete. I will

---

14 Wayne C. Booth, *The Rhetoric of Fiction*, 2nd ed. (University of Chicago Press, 1983), 441.

unpack that observation throughout this book. Abstractions rarely move, but a vivid image penetrates the heart. This is illustrated by the ancient Chinese story of a king who sees an ox being
led to slaughter.[15] The ox seems to sense its impending fate because it trembles pitiably. Moved with compassion, the king orders
the handlers to locate a sheep to be used in place of the ox. Later the king is criticized for being stingy—offering a sheep instead
of an ox. He explains that stinginess was not in play; rather, he
was moved because he *saw* the ox but not the sheep. Out of sight,
out of mind. Vivid, concrete language moves the heart like actual
images. In classical rhetoric this phenomenon was discussed with
the theories of *enargeia* (Greek) and *evidentia* (Latin). In the eigh-
teenth-century the Scottish professor and minister, George Campbell, called it "vivacity."[16]

| Operations of the Mind | Operations of the Mind |
| --- | --- |
| Direct Sensory Experience *(Most compelling)* | Actual Experience in Battle *(Most compelling)* |
| Memory of Direct Sensory Experience | Memory of Battle |
| Imagination of Direct Sensory Experience *(Less compelling)* | Language with Vivacity to Spark Imagination of Battle *(Less compelling)* |

*Figure 1.3: George Campbell's Theory of "Vivacity"*

Building on the brain science of the day, Campbell said that the
most compelling "operation of the mind" was *direct sensory experience*. This can be illustrated with a soldier on Iwo Jima. The
whizzing bullets commandeered the soldier's mind and compelled
involuntary attention. Next for Campbell was the *memory* of direct sensory experience. If the veteran of Iwo Jima has PTSD, he

---

15 Recounted in Chaim Perelman and L. Olbrechts-Tyteca, *The New Rhetoric: A Treatise on Argumentation* (University of Notre Dame Press, 1969), 116.

16 George Campbell, *The Philosophy of Rhetoric*, ed. Lloyd F. Bitzer (South-
ern Illinois University Press, 1988). A survey and critique of "vivacity," *enargeia*,
and *evidentia* can be found in the unpublished PhD dissertation of Michael
Howard Roth, "Cynosure: A Theoretical Grounding for Pictorial Language That
Grasps Attention" (Middlesex University/London School of Theology, 2018).

knows the power of memory. Next was *imagination* of direct sensory experience. Orators rarely use the first two operations of the mind. Instead, their tools are words that prompt imagination. For those words to be compelling they must have "vivacity." They must be vivid. Narrative is an ideal form of communication to leverage the attention-compelling, emotion-inducing power of vivid language. Virtually no one alive today has first-hand memories of Iwo Jima, but through stories we heard and films we have seen we can picture ourselves in the middle of the terrifying battle.

Narrative rhetoric works not only by being concrete, but also by leveraging the power of pathos or emotional proof.[17] The Bible includes emotion—along with perceptions, beliefs, and values—as part of the "heart." From the heart flow words and actions. Robert Baker proposes that "it is not unreasonable to assume that the Bible contains texts designed to evoke not just proper understanding (orthodoxy) or just proper actions (orthopraxy) but also proper feeling (orthopathy or orthokardia)."[18]

Yet another way narrative rhetoric works is by being indirect. Listeners react to stories differently than they do to arguments. When listeners are confronted with an argument, they raise the shields of counter-argument, but "Once upon a time," "And it came to pass," or "A certain rich man said" invite us to temporarily inhabit another world. In that world, sound theology and moral exhortations "steal past [the] watchful dragons."[19] The story of Absalom suspended between heaven and earth might work better than argument to convince a listener that revenge and pride are works of the devil. The story of Paul and Silas singing at midnight might work better than a three-point outline to inspire a listener to

---

17 For overviews of the importance of pathos in preaching and persuasion, see Ralph L. Lewis and Gregg Lewis, *Learning to Preach Like Jesus* (Crossway, 1989), 35–68; Jeffrey D. Arthurs, "The Place of Pathos in Preaching," *Journal of the Evangelical Homiletics Society* 1/1 (Dec. 2001): 1–10; Chip Heath and Dan Heath, *Made to Stick: Why Some Ideas Survive and Others Die* (Random House, 2007), 165–203.

18 Robert O. Baker, "Pentecostal Bible Reading: Toward a Model of Reading for the Formation of Christian Affections," *Journal of Pentecostal Theology* 7 (1995): 39.

19 C. S. Lewis, "Sometimes Fairy Stories May Say Best What's to be Said," *New York Times*, Book Review section (Nov. 18, 1956): 310.

rejoice always and remain faithful ever. In literary theory, stealing by the "dragons" is referred to as the *willing suspension of disbelief.* The concept applies mainly to fiction, but the same rhetorical dynamic is in play with history also.

May I offer one more observation on how narrative rhetoric works? Retention. The human mind has enormous capacity for the memory of pictures, and as we have seen, vivid language operates on the mind and emotions like pictures and sensory experience. To work *with* the brain rather than arm wrestling it with propositions, we might try communicating as the Bible does, with stories. This will help us employ what Jensen calls "stereo preaching," reaching both right and left brains.[20] Part Two offers multiple strategies for reaching both brains.

## Theologically Saturated

The genre of narrative is well-suited to convey the theological worldview that places God as the author, director, and lead actor of the play. In biblical narrative he is creator, redeemer, law-giver, and judge; father, mother, master, and husband; shepherd, potter, king, and warrior. Narrative is a supple genre to convey that God acts purposefully in the world he created.

Setting shows us where we are—in a paradise gone bad, wending our way to the celestial city. Character shows us who we are—God's crowning creation gone bad but redeemed and being progressively sanctified by his Spirit. Plot shows us what is wrong and what is the remedy—creation, fall, redemption, and consummation. As Alter states, theology is "entrammeled in history."[21] Old Testament narrators wrote with a compelling sense of theological purpose, for Israel was a "tiny often imperfectly monotheistic island in a vast and alluring sea of paganism."[22] The New Testament narrators had no less drive to write theology, for they observed God regathering his flock and opening the door of the fold

---

20 Richard A. Jensen, *Thinking in Story: Preaching in a Post-Literate Age* (CSS, 1995), 57.

21 Alter, *Art of Biblical Narrative*, 12.

22 Ibid., 155.

to form the church. The Spirit blew and the fledgling church flew the nest.

Yet in narrative, theology wears the garments of story—showing more than telling. The figure below illustrates the process of moving from exegetical details through the "homiletical idea" (the central idea of the sermon). The road must travel through theology. Four questions help us identify the author's theological intentions.

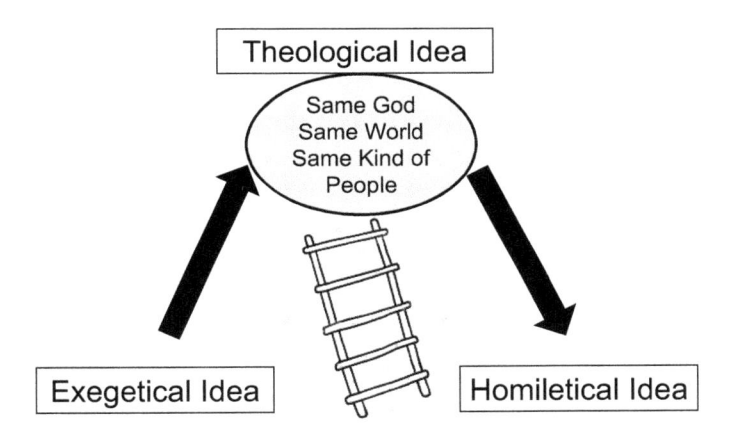

*Figure 1.4: Theological Idea*

**1. Does the narrator or a reliable character in the story explicitly reveal the theological point?** John 20:30–31 is a well-known example of this. John states plainly why he selected and narrated certain "signs" from the ministry of Jesus: "So that you may believe that Jesus is the Christ, the Son of God." This statement reveals that John was a theologian and rhetorician, seeking to persuade the readers to believe in order to receive life.

We have already seen in the story of David, Bathsheba, and Uriah that the narrator inserts himself into the flow of the plot with this comment: "The thing David had done displeased the Lord" (2 Sam 11:27). Sometimes an authoritative comment like this is stated by a character in the story rather than the narrator. When that character is Jesus or a prophet, the comment carries the same weight as if the omniscient narrator had made it. Luke 19:9–10 is an example. At the end of the story of Zacchaeus, Jesus announces to the crowd, "Today salvation has come to this house, since he also is a son of Abraham. For the Son of Man came to seek and to save the lost." By quoting Jesus, Luke takes us aside as if to say, "Did you get it? Jesus just summarized what this story shows. Being a true son of Abraham hinges on repentance and belief, and that's why I came to earth—to help people repent and believe."

When the narrator steps in to "tell" us the theological point, the task of interpretation is relatively easy, and it rests on solid ground. But narrators do not often "tell," do they? Read on.

**2. What theology does the narrator *show* rather than *tell*?** Here the interpretive ground is less firm, but as a means of conveying theology, the ambiguity of narrative is both a delight and a challenge. A delight because a narrative, like a riddle, teases the mind into active thought. To discern the character of God and his intentions for his world, we must ponder, following the signposts the narrator has staked. We worship the same God who is present throughout the Bible and in our time as well—the immutable, covenant-keeping God. We also inhabit the same world as the world of the Bible, although we must be quick to acknowledge the significant cultural differences between then and now. But this world is still a place of threat and security, pain and pleasure, a fallen Eden being remade. And we are the same kind of people as those in the Bible: saints and sinners, steadfast and faltering. The following list describes some signposts biblical narrators use to show theology:

- *Repetition.* Biblical narrative was produced and received in an oral culture. Words faded with the sound of the echo, rather than being calcified in print. In an oral culture repetition/restatement serves like a headline or italics in print communication. Returning to the example from 2 Samuel, we saw that the narrator drums the word "send." Another example of repetition is "voice" (Heb. *qol*) in 1 Samuel 15. You will remember that this is the story of Samuel confronting Saul for his disobedience. Saul did not completely annihilate the Amalekites as commanded. Most translations miss the significance of *qol* when they render verse 1 as, "Listen to the words of the Lord." More literally it should be, "Listen to the voice of the word of the Lord." "Voice" shows up again in the "bleating" of the sheep and "lowing" of the cattle (15:14), literally the "voice" of the sheep and cattle. Furthermore, Saul makes excuses for his disobedience by blaming the people: "I feared the people and listened to their voice" (15:24). Thus the author shows a contrast between attending to the voice of God and the voice of competing advice. When the repetition of "voice" is coupled with the repetition of "listen/obey" (*shama*), the author communicates that God demands complete attention and adherence to his word. I preached a sermon from this passage entitled, "Will You Not Listen?"

On a structural level, not just the level of individual words, the story of Balaam is remarkable for repetition and parallelism (Num 22–24).[23] Balak the Moabite hired Balaam the prophet to curse Israel. But God says to Balaam, "You shall not curse the people, for they are blessed" (22:12), and after the comical scene with the donkey, Balaam consents: "The word that God puts in my mouth, that must I speak" (22:38). So, three times Balaam instructs Balak to build seven altars and to sacrifice seven oxen and sheep. Balaam and Balak trundle from one vantage point to the next, but the formulaic rituals avail nothing. Balaam is unable to do anything except speak the word of the Lord, blessing those whom God has declared blessed. Thus the author *shows* how paganism, with its mechanistic worldview, its belief that divinity can be controlled by the techniques of a priestly caste, is merely laughable. As Alter states, in "the biblical perspective reality is in fact controlled by the will of an omnipotent God beyond all human manipulation."[24]

- *Climax.* The "point" of a story is most often revealed in the turning point. That is what we saw in the story of Zacchaeus. The climax occurs when Zacchaeus takes his stand and makes a speech, declaring that he is through extorting the people. The

---

23  Ibid., 104–107.
24  Ibid., 107.

author shows how an encounter with Jesus produces repentance and faith, and these make someone a true Israelite.

In the scene of baby Moses in the bulrushes (Exod 2:1–10), the climax occurs when Pharaoh's daughter rescues him and takes him into the palace as her own adopted child. The narrator comments laconically, "When the child grew older ... he became her son" (2:10). The hand has reached into the doll's house and is busy arranging things for the deliverance of enslaved Israel. Worded as a proposition, the meaning might be: God has not forgotten his enslaved people, but is actively orchestrating people and events to deliver them.

- *Volume.* By this I mean the number of words in a story dedicated to theme X or Y. In oral cultures, one way to emphasize an important theme is simply by devoting words to it. Unimportant things can be brushed over. To use an analogy: Rembrandt used very loose brushwork, almost like the style of later Impressionism, on backgrounds and clothing; but the face, and especially the eyes, were painted with vivid clarity. He wanted us to look at the face and eyes, so he labored over them. Just so, storytellers spend time on what they want us to look at. In Genesis, Joseph (and Joseph's sovereign, watchful God) receives many chapters (39–50), but the sun, moon, and stars receive only a paragraph (1:14–19). In 1 Kings 18, the showdown between Yahweh and Baal, the artist labors to paint in detail the power and attentiveness of Yahweh, especially as contrasted with the silence and impotence of Baal. The prophets of the Canaanite god cry out, cut themselves, and dance like dervishes around the altar, but "no one answered; no one paid attention" (18:29). Then Elijah methodically rebuilds the altar of the Lord, carefully prepares the sacrifice, douses it with twelve buckets of water, and prays a brief prayer. The reader has been held in suspense by all of this description, but then in the climax the fire of God falls, and the people provide the theological meaning of the story: "The Lord, he is God; the Lord, he is God" (18:38–39).

The next two points overlap with the previous material, but I think it will be helpful to make these explicit as we see how biblical narrators convey theology.

**3. What is the "vision of God" in the text?**[25] Is God omnipotent, omniscience, reliable, or merciful? Is he immanent, kind, frustrated, or protective? What does the author show? In Matthew 1:18–25 the author shows us the God who works miracles in sending his Son. Mary is found to be with child from the Holy Spirit. This story is the first narrative "argument" in a series of scenes about the unique person of Jesus. While I believe that biblical narratives offer ethical instruction as well as theology (see the section below), it would be a mistake to turn this passage into something like "lessons for engaged couples." That was not Matthew's primary intention.

**4. What is the "fallen condition focus"?** This question arises from the work of Bryan Chapell.[26] He calls this exegetical probe the "FCF," and it is corollary to the previous question about God. Here we ask about humans—what aspect of fallenness does the author show, and what gracious provision has he provided to meet that need? As stated earlier in this chapter, we and the people of the Bible are the "same kind of people," and the FCF helps us identify "the mutual human condition that contemporary believers share with those" in the story or those to whom the story was written.[27]

The FCF relates to sins such as pride (Herod who was eaten with worms, Acts 12:20–23); cowardice and prejudice (Peter who refused to eat with Gentiles, Gal 2:11–14); and worldliness (Solomon who married foreign wives and turned from the Lord, 1 Kgs 11). It also includes aspects of living in a broken world that are not necessarily sinful: our finite, fragile, and faltering condition.[28] The man who lamented, "I believe; help my unbelief" was not necessarily sinning, but he was faltering (Mark 9:24). Paul and Silas in the stocks were not sinning (Acts 16), but persecution certainly reminds us of our fragile state and tempts us to falter. Naomi

---

25 Haddon W. Robinson, *Biblical Preaching: The Development and Delivery of Expository Messages*, 3rd ed. (Baker, 2014), 64–65.

26 Bryan Chapell, *Christ-Centered Preaching: Redeeming the Expository Sermon*, 2nd ed. (Baker, 2005), 48–54.

27 Ibid., 50.

28 Zack Eswine, *Preaching to a Post-Everything World: Crafting Sermons that Connect with Our Culture* (Baker, 2008), 45–48.

and Ruth were finite and fragile as they dragged into Bethlehem (Ruth 1–2).

Consideration of the vision of God and the FCF leads naturally to the next aspect of biblical narrative: the authors intended their stories not only to inform us about God and humanity, but they also intended the stories to transform us.

### Intended for Edification

Biblical narrative is a mighty tool to save unbelievers and build up believers. As biblical narrative reveals theology, it simultaneously draws ethical implications. We see this in Deuteronomy 26:5–10:

> A wandering Aramean was my father. And he went down into Egypt and sojourned there, few in number, and there he became a nation, great, mighty, and populous. And the Egyptians treated us harshly and humiliated us and laid on us hard labor. Then we cried to the Lord... . And the Lord brought us out of Egypt with a mighty hand and an outstretched arm, with great deeds of terror, with signs and wonders. And he brought us into this place and gave us this land... . And behold, now I bring the first of the fruit of the ground, which you, O Lord, have given me.

Psalm 136, one of the storytelling psalms, takes a similar approach. It goes all the way back to creation (vv. 4–9), then to the plagues in Egypt and the parting of the Red Sea (vv. 10–15), then to the wilderness and eventually to the Promised Land (vv. 16–22). The moral of the story? "Give thanks to the God of heaven, for his steadfast love endures forever" (v. 26).

In addition to providing the rationale for obedience, the stories of the Hebrew Bible give models for behavior. The stories are to be read in light of the Mosaic Law as illustrations of righteous and unrighteous attitudes and actions. For example, the author clearly intended for the readers to evaluate Absalom's flattery, manipulation, and rebellion in a negative light (2 Sam 13–15). Absalom walked in the path of sinners. No wonder he was like the chaff that the wind drove away.

The New Testament authors use the Old Testament stories as guides for behavior. In 1 Corinthians 10 Paul summarizes nine stories of the Exodus to draw this principle: "These things took place as examples for us, that we might not desire evil as they did" (v. 6). Jesus urged his disciples, "Remember Lot's wife," as an example of what will happen in the coming persecution: "Whoever seeks to preserve his life will lose it" (Luke 17:32–33). Similarly, John states bluntly, "We should not be like Cain, who was of the evil one and murdered his brother" (1 John 3:12). Hebrews gives us models of faith (chapter 11), James says we should pray fervently as did Elijah (5:15–18), and Jesus used the example of David to show the Pharisees that Sabbath-keeping is a matter of the spirit more than a matter of the oral law. David ate the bread of the Presence even though that action was not strictly lawful (Matt 12:1–8).

The edificational purpose of biblical narrative is quite in keeping with ancient historiography which was, as Witherington states, "Mainly hortatory in character." It was "meant to teach lessons to audiences and inform not merely their views but their behavior. In other words, ancient biographies were exercises in persuasion, using storytelling and speeches to accomplish their aims."[29] In the schools of rhetoric in the Greco-Roman world, an elementary exercise was to write historical vignettes called "chreia"—short character-revealing and character-forming sketches from the lives of great men. The ancient storytellers knew that narrative can be a powerful force for edification.

The edificational function of narrative is simply part of the nature of the genre. Narrators overtly or covertly make moral appraisals on events and characters and write in ways that seek to convince readers. This is simply part of what happens when real events are turned into narrative. As Amos Wilder puts it, all stories "posit a scheme or order in the nowhere of the world."[30] Through the narratives of the Bible, the community of believers learns its values: lying

---

29 Ben Witherington III, *New Testament Rhetoric: An Introductory Guide to the Art of Persuasion in and of the New Testament* (Cascade, 2009), 24.

30 Amos Wilder, "Story and Story-World," *Interpretation* 37 (1983): 360.

is bad, honesty is good; adultery is wrong, chastity is right; faith is to be emulated, cowardice is to be rejected, and so forth.

One way to look at the nature of biblical narrative as both theology and moral example is with Fee and Stuart's "three levels of meaning."[31]

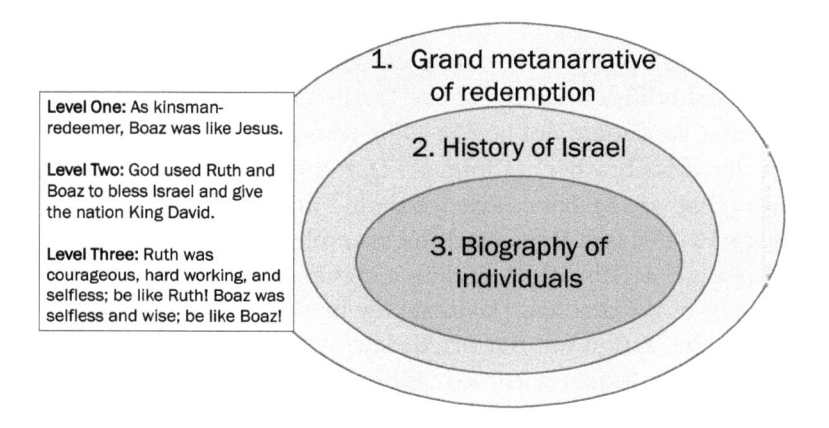

Level One: As kinsman-redeemer, Boaz was like Jesus.

Level Two: God used Ruth and Boaz to bless Israel and give the nation King David.

Level Three: Ruth was courageous, hard working, and selfless; be like Ruth! Boaz was selfless and wise; be like Boaz!

1. Grand metanarrative of redemption

2. History of Israel

3. Biography of individuals

*Figure 1.5: Three Levels of Meaning*

*Top level.* Every Old Testament story contributes to the grand narrative of creation, fall, redemption, and consummation. Every story can be legitimately interpreted in light of its place in the metanarrative. When Jesus stated that the Scriptures "bear witness about me" (John 5:39) he was speaking about the top level, as was Luke who summarized the conversation on the Emmaus Road: "Beginning with Moses and the all the Prophets, he interpreted to them in all the Scriptures the things concerning himself" (Luke 24: 27). Thus, when we read that Boaz was a "kinsman-redeemer" (Heb. *go'el*) we see a beautiful analog to Jesus the ultimate redeemer. Sometimes the top level is called "redemptive history," and the Apostles often read their Bibles—what we call the "Old Testament"—this way. In fact, 1 Corinthians 10, which I cited above to demonstrate that the Apostles drew moral lessons from the ancient narratives, also interprets the narratives Christologically. Paul says

---

31 Gordon D. Fee and Douglas Stuart, *How the Read the Bible for All Its Worth*, third edition (Zondervan, 2003), 91–92.

that the Israelites who grumbled in the wilderness "put Christ to the test" (v. 9); and when they drank water that came from the rock that Moses struck, "the Rock was Christ" (v. 4).

In the field of homiletics, discussions of Christ-centered preaching, have proliferated since the early 2000s. Dyed-in-the-wool advocates argue that *every* passage and *every* sermon *must* talk primarily about Jesus and not about humanity. They contrast Christ-centered preaching with "moralistic" or "moral exemplar" preaching ("be like David," "don't be like David"). The stance that I take in this book is both-and, not either-or.[32] The narratives of the Bible do reveal theology, including Christology, and they also provide models of behavior. With staunch Christ-centered advocates I recoil from moralism in sermons, implying that we have the ability to win God's favor by our good behavior rather than his grace; but I do not recoil from moral formation. I do contend that God is the ultimate protagonist in biblical narrative; but humans are also present in and indispensable to those narratives. Returning to the example above from Matthew 1 (Mary conceiving the Christ), I resist turning that story into "lessons for engaged couples"; nevertheless, the author does point out that Joseph is a "just" (righteous) man who acted humbly and gently toward his betrothed. In that sense, he is a good example for fiancés and all of us. All Scripture is "profitable for teaching, for reproof, for correction, and for training in righteousness" (2 Tim 3:16).

*Middle level.* This is the history of Israel, and every Old Testament story plays a role on this level as well. Each story shows a facet of how God redeemed a people to honor his name. Thus Boaz acting as kinsman-redeemer, and Ruth acting courageously, loyally, and selflessly to save Naomi, became the forebears of mighty King David. A genealogy linking Boaz to David concludes the book and reveals that the author was thinking on the "middle level."

---

32 My approach is similar to the one offered by Steven D. Mathewson in *The Art of Preaching Old Testament Narrative*, second edition (Baker, 2021), 15–26. Mathewson summarizes the history and main players in the debate between exemplar preaching and Christ-centered preaching. See also Kenneth Langley, "Theocentric View," in *Homiletics and Hermeneutics: Four Views on Preaching Today*, ed. Scott M. Gibson and Matthew D. Kim (Baker, 2018), 81–106.

*Bottom level.* From the Bible's hundreds of individual biographies and vignettes, preachers can discern moral lessons, either positive or negative, intended by the author. Just remember that when you use narrative on this level, it should be interpreted in light of the top level and folded into it as you preach. For example, when preaching on Joseph and Mary, keep the main thing the main thing—the miraculous birth of Jesus; and then if you desire, feel free to point out that Joseph was a good man. God used his obedience in the great plan of the incarnation, and he inspires us to obedience as well.

Thank you for flying with me at a high altitude. Let's descend now for a look at the four key features of biblical narrative—plot, character, setting, and point of view. Then we will be ready to consider how to reproduce those dynamics in our sermons.

## For Further Study

- Alter, Robert. *The Art of Biblical Narrative.* Basic Books, 1981.
- Fee, Gordon D. Fee and Stuart, Douglas. *How the Read the Bible for All Its Worth.* 3rd ed. Zondervan, 2003.
- Kuhn, Karl Allen. *The Heart of Biblical Narrative: Rediscovering Biblical Appeal to the Emotions.* Fortress, 2009.
- Mathewson, Steven D. *The Art of Preaching Old Testament Narrative.* 2nd ed. Baker, 2021.
- Rhoads, David, Joanna Dewey, and Donald Michie. *Mark as Story: An Introduction to the Narrative of a Gospel.* 2nd ed. Fortress, 1999.
- Ryken, Leland. *How to Read the Bible as Literature.* Zondervan, 1984.

## *Talk about It*

Which do you find easier to communicate when preaching from narrative—theology or ethics? That is, do you tend toward doxology or exhortation? Why? Is your tendency a problem or a strength?

## Dig Deeper

Listen to a podcast that structures its material as a narrative, perhaps "This American Life" or "Invisibilia." Notice how they keep the plot moving forward yet pause every now and then for commentary. Could this be one way you might preach biblical narrative—primarily story, but with commentary sprinkled in?

## Practice

To get the hang of working with Robinson's concept of "the vision of God," write a list of God's attributes from the stories of Nadab and Abihu (Lev 10), the report of the spies who scoped out the Promised Land (Num 13), or the bronze serpent (Num 21). Do the same for the FCF ("fallen condition focus"). What do these stories show about humans when they walk apart from God?

# 2

# Plot

*"No, no! The adventures first," said the
Gryphon in an impatient tone: "explana-
tions take such dreadful time."*[1]

Lewis Carroll

*Only trouble is interesting. This is not so
in life.*[2]

Charles Baxter

C HAPTER 1 WAS a general introduction to the art of
narrative, and now it is time to get into specifics. Of the
four elements of the genre—plot, character, setting, and
point of view—plot is first among equals. Aristotle called it the
"soul of tragedy" and "the most important thing."[3] This is because,
as we will see below, the primary way narrators convey ideas and
engage the audience is by hooking us with a dilemma and working it out through a sequence of events. Simply stated, we want to
know "what happens next?" Much of the magic of narrative lies in
that simple, universally experienced, question.

Although this chapter puts plot on center stage, I want to affirm

---

1 *Alice's Adventures in Wonderland*, quoted in Jeanine K. Brown, *The Gospels as Stories: A Narrative Approach to Matthew, Mark, Luke, and John* (Baker,
2020), 21.

2 In Jonathan Gottschall, *The Storytelling Animal: How Stories Make Us Human* (Mariner Books, 2013), 52.

3 Aristotle, *The Poetics*, 1450a, 1450b; trans. W. Rhys Roberts and Ingram
Bywater (Random House, 1984), 232, 233.

that the four components of the genre form an organic whole. Plot is a summary of the actions *characters* take. Brooks and Warren state simply that plot is "character in action."[4] Similarly, *setting* establishes the place and conditions of what happens in the plot. And *point of view* pervades all of these. Only dissection can separate the elements of the genre, but in a descriptive task like exegesis, isolating and labeling the components helps us identify what the author is saying and doing.

## What Is Plot?

Aristotle said that a story should have a beginning, middle, and end; and in the long history of literary theory, the discussion of plot has basically restated, clarified, and expanded his modest insight. But plenty of DNA is packed into the nucleus of Aristotle's statement. The sidebar catalogs a handful of definitions of "plot" that in one way or another rest on Aristotle's *Poetics*. As we contemplate the soul of narrative, I will describe plot under two headings—causality and conflict—and I'll use the stories of Elijah on Mount Carmel and Zacchaeus in the tree as running examples.

| |
|---|
| The plan, design, scheme of pattern of events.... The organization of incident and character in such as way as to induce curiosity and suspense.<br>J. Cuddon, *A Dictionary of Literary Terms* (Penguin, 1984), s.v. "plot." |
| A series of events around a central conflict and possessing a unified development.<br>Leland Ryken, *The Literature of the Bible* (Zondervan, 1974), 26. |
| Events—their order in the narrative, sequential relations, turning points and breakthroughs, and the development and resolution of conflicts.<br>Rhoads, Dewey, and Michie, *Mark As Story: An Introduction to the Narrative of a Gospel*, 2nd ed. (Fortress, 1999), 6. |
| The moving suspense of a story from disequilibrium to resolution.<br>Eugene L. Lowry, *Doing Time in the Pulpit: The Relationship Between Narrative and Preaching* (Abingdon, 1985), 52. |

---

4 Cleanth Brooks and Robert Penn Warren, *Understanding Fiction* (Appleton-Century-Croft, 1959), 80.

| |
|---|
| The chain of events in a story and the principle which knits it together.<br>Edwin Muir, *The Structure of the Novel* (Hogarth, 1963), 16. |
| The linear development of the events which carry conflict, suspense, and a resolution.<br>James Freedman, "Samson's Dry Bones: A Structural Reading of Judges 13–16," in *Literary Interpretations of Biblical Narratives*, ed. Kenneth Gros Louis (Abingdon, 1982), 105. |

*Figure 2.1: Definitions of "Plot"*

## Causality

Novelist and literary critic E. M. Forster coined what has become a maxim in literary theory: "'The king died and then the queen died' is a story. 'The king died and then the queen died of grief' is a plot."[5] He meant, of course, that causality is indispensable to plot. One event must cause, modify, or exert some force on the following event. Forster uses the word "story" to mean "chronicle," a bald recounting of events arranged in time sequence but with little connection between the events. In contrast to a story/chronicle, "a plot is also a narrative of events, the emphasis falling on causality."[6]

To take an example from biblical narrative: with hubris Peter overestimates his commitment to the Lord, *then* at the charcoal fire he is given an opportunity to demonstrate the loyalty he trumpeted, *then* he denies that he even knows Jesus, *then* he is grief-stricken, *then* Jesus restores him, *then* he is filled with the Holy Spirit, *then* he becomes the leader of the church. As the plot thickens, the range of what could happen next is narrowed by the previous event. In Paul Goodman's oft-quoted reflection on Aristotle: "In the beginning anything is possible; in the middle things become probable, in the ending everything is necessary."[7] The path leads home. It is teleological, illuminating the beginning by the end.

The events that lead to Elijah on Mount Carmel begin *in medias*

---

5  E. M. Forster, *Aspects of the Novel* (Penguin, 1927), 93.

6  Ibid., 93.

7  Paul Goodman, *The Structure of Literature* (University of Chicago Press, 1954), 14; quoted in James L. Resseguie, *Narrative Criticism of the New Testament: An Introduction* (Baker, 2005), 198.

*res* ("into the middle of things"). Elijah has already had plenty of conflict with wicked King Ahab when the Lord sends him to announce a showdown: "You have abandoned the commandments of the Lord and followed the Baals. Now therefore send and gather all Israel to me at Mount Carmel, and the 450 prophets of Baal and the 400 prophets of Asherah who eat at Jezebel's table" (1 Kgs 18:18–19). The prophets gather, *then* Elijah challenges the people to choose whom they will follow, *then* he lays out the conditions of the test (a trial by fire), *then* the prophets call on the name of their god from morning until noon but receive only silence, *therefore* Elijah mocks them, *so* in a final paroxysm of devotion they cut themselves with swords and lances, *but still* "there was no voice" (v. 29), *then* Elijah prepares his altar and sacrifice, *then* to make sure the people have no doubts about the power of Yahweh he douses the sacrifice repeatedly, *then* he prays a short prayer, *in response* the fire of God falls. It "consumed the burnt offering and the wood and the stones and the dust, and licked up the water that was in the trench" (v. 38). *Accordingly* the people fell on their faces before the true God.

The opening conflict between Yahweh and Baal (and their representatives Elijah and Ahab) has escalated and been resolved step by step. The author of 1 Kings has brought us home.

Luke does the same with the story of Zacchaeus. This story also begins *in medias res* as Jesus works his way to Jerusalem for the final time. He enters Jericho where a man by the name of Zacchaeus wants to see him, *but* he cannot because he is short, *so* he runs ahead and climbs a tree, *then* Jesus stops under the tree and invites himself to Zacchaeus's house, *this causes* the crowd to grumble, *then* Zacchaeus repents, *as a result* Jesus pronounces salvation on this lost sheep he has rescued.

## Conflict

This indispensable element of plot is implied in the point above. Conflict is the problem that is worked out through the series of causally-related events. It is the "heart of story, the principle of its form and the genius of its power."[8] The conflict may be physical,

---

8 Eugene L. Lowry, *Doing Time in the Pulpit: The Relationship Between*

emotional, moral, or spiritual. It may be external or internal. It may take place between individuals, or between individuals and groups, or even between individuals and themselves as they wrestle with a moral dilemma. When it comes to narratives in the Bible, we should remember that all conflicts ultimately are a matter of "good versus evil," or even "God versus the devil." Whatever form the conflict embodies, the narrative takes flight when the protagonist finds himself or herself in a pickle, and the plane lands when the problem is resolved. If it is resolved to the benefit of the protagonist, the story is a "comedy," and if it turns out poorly for the protagonist, it is a "tragedy." The terms "protagonist" and "antagonist" have the Greek word *agon* ("struggle," "contest") as their root, and this reminds us that conflict is the core of narrative.

The figure below lists types of conflict in biblical narrative.

| Type | Examples |
| --- | --- |
| Person versus person | David v. Goliath, Sarai persecutes Hagar |
| Person versus God (or supernatural being) | Jonah runs from God, Jacob wrestles with the angel |
| Person versus group | Moses v. the Israelites, Jesus v. the Pharisees |
| Person versus self | Gideon in the winepress, Jesus in the Garden |
| Person versus nature | The Israelites in the wilderness, the disciples in the storm |

*Figure 2.2: Types of Conflict*

I find it helpful when doing exegesis to lay out the plot visually, and the following figures offer three diagrams for doing so. The first is my own. The next one, the "Monomythic Cycle," is based on the theory of archetypes from literary critic Northrop Frye and has been adapted by screenwriter Robert McKee and homiletician Kent Edwards.[9] The "Homiletical Plot" is Eugene Lowry's

---

*Narrative and Preaching* (Abingdon, 1985), 55.

9 Northrop Frye, *Anatomy of Criticism: Four Essays* (Princeton University Press, 1957), 163–239; Robert McKee, *Story* (Regan, 1997); J. Kent Edwards,

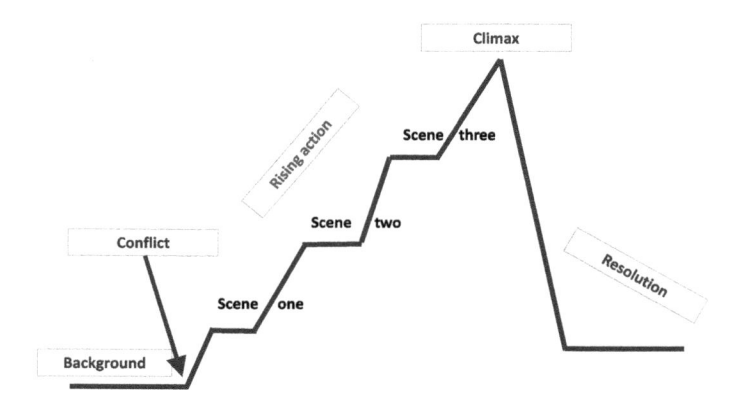

*Figure 2.3: Visualizing Plot Structure*

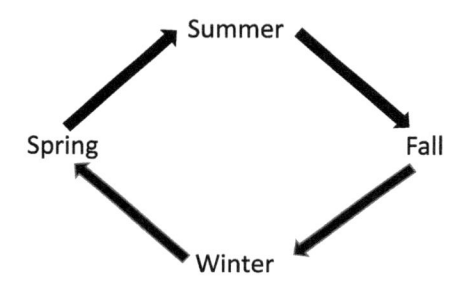

*Figure 2.4: Visualizing Plot Structure, the Monomythic Cycle*

concept.[10] Plot structure—the skeleton of the story—is universal, appearing throughout history and across cultures. To be sure, the "skeleton is somewhat cartilaginous—there is flex in it. But the flex is limited."[11]

---

*Effective First-Person Biblical Preaching: The Steps from Text to Narrative Sermon* (Zondervan, 2005), 41–52. The monomythic cycle typically begins in the Summer when all is well, but then a problem is introduced and the story bends downward to Fall. The nadir is depicted in Winter, but then the climax occurs, and the story bends upward to the Spring, a new state of equilibrium.

10 Eugene L. Lowry, *The Homiletical Plot: The Sermon as Narrative Art Form,* expanded ed. (John Knox, 2001), 27–87.

11 Gottschall, *The Storytelling Animal,* 52.

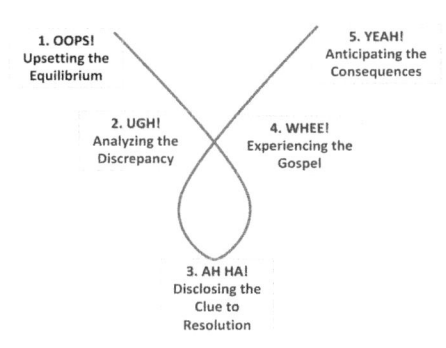

*Figure 2.5: Visualizing Plot Structure, Lowry's Homiletical Plot*

**Background** introduces the protagonist, establishes the setting, and provides information the listener needs to understand what comes next. Conflict has not yet occurred (although it may be hinted at), so this stage of the plot just sets up the dominoes before pushing over the first one. In a fairytale, the background might begin, "Once upon a time," or "A long time ago in a galaxy far, far away." In the story of Elijah and the prophets of Baal, 1 Kings 18:20 says, "So Ahab sent to all the people of Israel and gathered the prophets together at Mount Carmel." Then in verse 21 Elijah challenges the people to stop limping between two opinions—God or Baal—and the story is off and running.

In Luke 19, the background is presented in verses 1–2: Jesus was passing through Jericho and there was a rich man there named Zacchaeus. He was a chief tax collector. Notice that even here tension starts to rise, or at least curiosity: "A chief tax collector lived there? I wonder how Jesus will respond to him. This ought to be a story worth hearing!"

The **conflict** is often stated or implied in just a verse or two. I have pictured that in the diagram by making the conflict an arrow that indicates a point in time. Normally this occurs near the beginning of the story, but in 1 Kings 18:20–40, the conflict occurs in the previous verses in the chapter: Elijah versus Ahab and his false prophets. As we saw in Chapter One, biblical narrative is imbued with theology and ethics, so what looks like a showdown between the prophet and the king is actually a fight between Yahweh and

Baal. As you know, the contest ends up being completely one-sided, and therein lies the theological purpose of the author—to contrast the reality and power of the true God with the chimera of the false gods.

In Luke 19 the conflict is stated in verse 3: Zacchaeus "was seeking to see who Jesus was." The conflict is modest, not imbued with pyrotechnics like Yahweh verses Baal, but there is more here than meets the eye. As I stated above, even prior to the statement about wanting to see Jesus, the reader already feels tension because Zacchaeus was a notorious sinner (v. 2). Will Jesus befriend him? Furthermore, Luke has repeatedly reminded the reader that Jesus is headed to Jerusalem. He is on a mission to lay down his life. Will he have time for one more lost sheep? The unremarkable verb, Zacchaeus wanted to "see" Jesus, may imply more than curiosity. It may suggest that the tax collector is a seeker, wanting to encounter and connect to Jesus. The rising action (covered next) shows the desperate actions of someone who truly did want to "see" Jesus.

The **rising action** is the longest portion of the story, as represented in the diagram. I have drawn this portion in stair steps. Each step is a scene or complication in the story. The line progresses up and up, suggesting that the listeners feel more and more tension as they approach the turning point. Classic stories (and jokes) have three stair steps, as in the parable of the Good Samaritan, but that is not a hard and fast rule for narratives, so do not be misled by the diagram. A story could have two scenes, or three, or more. In Elijah versus Ahab, there are many complications:

- Elijah stands alone, but the prophets of Baal are 450 (v. 22).
- The false prophets call on their deities to send consuming fire (vv. 23–29). Note: this stair step could be sub-divided because the author loads many details here and uses vivid language that slows the experience of reading, such as the false prophets' manic gyrations to get their god's attention. If the author of 1 Kings had been a movie maker this portion might have been filmed with close up or slow motion. If he had been Rembrandt, he would have painted these details with painstaking detail.

- Elijah repairs the altar and (perhaps) builds a second altar with twelve stones (vv. 30–32a).
- Elijah prepares a trench around the altar, laying the sacrifice on the wood, and soaking the whole mass (vv. 32b–35).
- Elijah prays (vv. 36–37).

In the story of Zacchaeus, his desire to see Jesus is complicated by his profession as a chief tax collector, shortness of stature, the desperation that caused him to run and climb a tree (activities for boys, not for important men of the community in first-century Israel), and the grumbling of the crowd. The reader wants to know what happens next—will Jesus stand up to the crowd and accept the prodigal returning home?

The **climax** is the turning point in the story, the breaking point, and shows how things turn out for the protagonist—comedy or tragedy. Like the statement of conflict, it too occurs in a brief period of time, in a verse or two. The story of Elijah has an exceptionally clear climax as the fire of God "fell and consumed the burnt offering and the wood and the stones and the dust, and licked up the water that was in the trench" (v. 38). The story of Zacchaeus is also clear: "Today salvation has come to this house" (v. 9). Zacchaeus truly has "seen" Jesus, and the experience has turned him around.

After the climax not much is left to tell, just the aftermath. This is called the **resolution** or **denouement**. The diagram shows the tension of the story falling sharply as the melody returns to the tonic chord, "And they lived happily ever after." Notice that the diagram ends at a slightly higher level than it began, indicating that although the crisis is resolved and winter has given way to spring, we can never return to the exact starting point. Conflict and resolution carry consequences after the action terminates. In 1 Kings 18 the people have seen Baal unmasked like the Wizard of Oz behind the curtain, and they fall to the ground affirming, "The Lord, he is God; the Lord, he is God." They seize the false prophets and slaughter them at the brook Kishon (vv. 39–40). Ahab is one step closer to reaching his ignominious downfall.

In Luke 19 Jesus sums up the whole incident with this

theologically rich statement: "For the Son of Man has come to seek and to save the lost" (v. 10). That is what Luke has showed us. He selected this event out of thousands of possible events to communicate that idea.

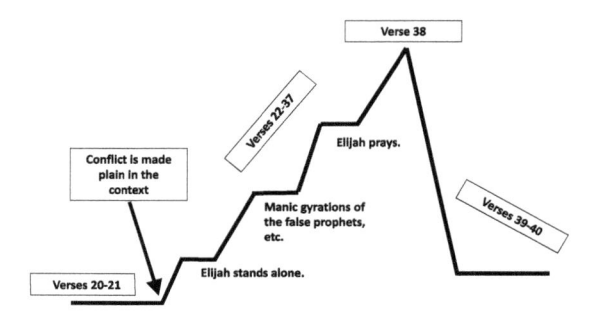

Figure 2.6: 1 Kings 18:20–40

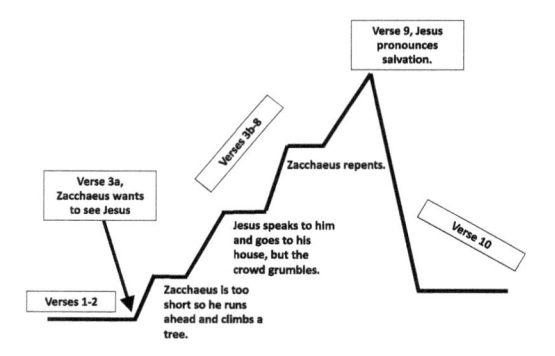

Figure 2.7: Luke 19:1–10

Stories nearly always have a clear climax and resolution, but not every story ends that way. The skeleton can flex by using an unresolved plot. This leaves the reader scratching his or her head with the haunting feeling that things are not tidied up. When used purposefully, an unresolved plot is powerful rhetoric that prompts the reader to "finish" the story.

The ultimate example of this is the ending of Mark (assuming that the "long ending" was not intended by the original author): Jesus has risen! The angel announces the good news to Mary Magdalene, Mary the mother of James, and Salome. Good news, right? Not so fast. In the final verse of the book we read that "they … fled from the tomb, for trembling and astonishment had seized them, and they said nothing to anyone, for they were afraid" (Mark 16:8). They said nothing to anyone? The symphony has climaxed, but instead of a resounding "Tum Tum ta Dum!" the final "ta Dum" is missing. The boat has arrived at shore, but as the readers disembark, they find no footing. This causes them to ponder the unsatisfying conclusion, and place themselves into the story: "They told no one? That doesn't seem right. I hope I would do better."

The book of Jonah is similar. The story ends with a rhetorical question that God asks pouting Jonah: "And should I not pity Nineveh, that great city, in which there are more than 120,000 persons who do not know their right hand from their left, and also much cattle?" (Jonah 4:11). Readers are drawn in to answer the question, make a judgment on Jonah's hard heart, and in the process judge their own hearts—do I align with God's values, or am I like Jonah?

Less charged but still rhetorically effective is the book of Acts. The gospel has advanced all the way to Rome and shows no signs of slowing down even though persecution dogs it. While in house arrest, Paul "welcomed all who came to him, proclaiming the kingdom of God and teaching about the Lord Jesus Christ with all boldness and without hindrance" (28:30–31). Luke ends his two-volume set with an ellipsis, implying that the good news will march on "to the end of the earth" (Acts 1:8).

Individual pericopes sometimes end without clear climax and resolution as with the rich young man who went away sorrowful because he had great possessions (Mark 10:22). The ending leaves the reader with a haunting sense that the young man will not live "happily ever after," and this moves listeners to tie up the loose ends in our own minds.

To help your congregation feel the power of unresolved plot, you might prepare a Scripture reading from 2 Kings:

- In the fiftieth year of Azariah king of Judah, Pekahiah the son of Menahem began to reign over Israel in Samaria.... *And he did what was evil in the sight of the Lord* (15:23–24).
- In the fifty-second year of Azariah king of Judah, Pekah the son of Remaliah began to reign over Israel in Samaria.... *And he did what was evil in the sight of the Lord.* (15:27–28)
- In the seventeenth year of Pekah the son of Remaliah, Ahaz the son of Jotham, king of Judah, began to reign.... *And he did not do what was right in the eyes of the Lord his God.* (16:1–2).
- Etc.

Many years ago, I heard such a Scripture reading, and I still remember the impact. A small group of gifted readers voiced the script so that the whole cast pounded the refrain in unison: "And he did what was evil in the sight of the Lord." This helped the listeners grasp the metronymic decline of God's people and yearn for a true king who would end the story the way it should be ended.

## The Rhetoric of Plot

The discussion of unresolved plot and the way it leaves listeners suspended leads to a discussion of the power of plot. Much of the rhetorical charm lies in the emotional experience pictured in the diagrams as the story drives to a climax or revolves from summer to winter and back to summer.

### Emotional Engagement

As a literary art form, narrative is unsurpassed in its ability to prompt emotional engagement. It rivals music that carries listeners through a melodic line, with unresolved and resolved chords, crescendos, decrescendos, and ritardandos. In particular, narrative has no rival in building suspense. The sequence of events makes listeners vicarious participants in the action. Aristotle implies this when he speaks of plot as "tying" and "loosening" (*Poetics*, 1455b). Readers' emotions are wound tight, then unwound, as the plot moves to resolution. Similarly, Culpepper states, "A plot requires a change of some kind, and its peculiar affective power is produced by the hopes and fears, desires and expectations it imposes on the reader as it unfolds from beginning to end."[12] My diagram of plot pictures this affective power as the rising action ascends step-by-step. We wonder if Gideon will win with only three hundred men. We quake with Jacob as Esau approaches. We are satisfied when Jezebel is overthrown. Narrative has great affective power and plot is largely responsible for this.

But what if the listeners already know how the story ends, so that there is no tension? They already know who "wins." This is, after all, the case with many church audiences and the well-known stories of the Bible. Fear not—the magic of plot still works. I have seen the original *Star Wars* movie a dozen times, and I know that Luke will blow up the Death Star, but I still like to watch it happen. I have seen Romeo and Juliet three or four times, and I still want Juliet to wake up in time to save Romeo, even though I know that's not going to happen. So, the emotional engagement of the plot does not depend only on suspense. It also draws on what rhetorician Kenneth Burke called "form." Even when listeners know where the road leads, they still want to travel it to the end. Burke puts it this way: "The arrows of our desires are turned in a certain direction, and the plot follows the direction of the arrows."[13] When that happens, the listeners experience satisfaction. If the story is well told, the formal excellence of the plot structure, like the formal excellence of an unresolved chord giving way to a resolved one, virtually guarantees that listeners will still be caught up in the story. Thus, there is no need for preachers to avoid the familiar stories of the Bible. Furthermore, in our day of shrinking biblical literacy, we can be sure that some attenders will not yet have heard the stories for the first time.

## Comprehension

Another rhetorical effect of plot relates to comprehension. Stories

---

12  R. Alan Culpepper, *Anatomy of the Fourth Gospel: A Study in Literary Design* (Fortress, 1983), 81.

13  Kenneth Burke, *Counter-Statement* (University of California Press, 1968), 124.

are easy to   follow because they flow chronologically. We find it difficult to follow the twists and turns of a logical argument, and even more difficult to remember it later, but nearly everyone can follow and remember a plot: first this happened, then this, then this. In Part Two, I will demonstrate how to organize our sermons similarly.

## Indirection

Yet another rhetorical effect takes us back to theology which is conveyed by *showing* and *telling*. Biblical narrative does lots of the former and enough of the latter to keep us on track with interpretation. Thus, narrative is a supple medium for narrative-theologians to present humanity's problems and God's provisions. Michael Root even argues that plotting in biblical narrative corresponds to soteriology because theories of the atonement have at core a movement from the problem of sin to the solution of redemption.[14] C. S. Lewis makes a related observation about fictional stories: "The plot ... is really only a net whereby to catch something else. The real theme ... usually is something that has no sequence to it, something other than a process and much more like a state or quality."[15] Through the rhetorical magic of plot, the author woos the readers to accept his depiction of humanity and God. We simultaneously sympathize and cringe with Jonah's hard heart, and we want to align our values with God's. When we see Leah place her self-worth in her relationship with Jacob, we come to see that only God can ultimately fill the emptiness we feel.

Biblical narrative catches protagonists not in the mundane tasks of life but at critical junctures.[16] These defining moments of-

---

14 Michael Root, "The Narrative Structure of Soteriology," pp. 263–273 in *Why Narrative: Readings in Narrative Theology*, ed. Stanley Hauerwas and L. Gregory Jones (Wipf and Stock, 1997).

15  C. S. Lewis, "On Stories" in *Essays Presented to Charles Williams*, ed. C. S. Lewis (1947; Eerdmans, 1966), 103.

16  Robert Alter has proposed the theory of "scene-types" to describe those moments: annunciation, birth (especially birth to a barren mother), encounter at a well, epiphany in a field, initiatory trial, danger and sustenance in the desert, and the testament of a dying hero. These scenes seem to have been familiar

ten involve a crisis, and in the climax the author offers the readers a vision of God that is the solution to the fallen condition. In the case of Elijah on Mount Carmel, the crisis occurs on a mountain (often a literary symbol of special insight about God), and the climax of the story makes plain, even without authorial commentary, that God is God and Baal is not. When Jesus passes through Jericho, we rejoice to see that he came to seek and save scoundrels like Zacchaeus. Maybe there is hope for us too!

## For Further Study

- Crane, R. S. "The Concept of Plot." Pages 233–243 in *Approaches to the Novel: Materials for a Poetics*. Edited by Robert Scholes. Chandler, 1966.
- Green, Barbara. "The Plot of the Biblical Story of Ruth." *Journal for the Study of the Old Testament* 23 (1982): 55–68.
- Kuhn, Karl Allen. *The Heart of Biblical Narrative: Rediscovering Biblical Appeal to the Emotions*. Fortress, 2009.

### Talk about It

Do you agree with Aristotle and Arthurs that plot is first among equals—the most important generic element? Explain your answer.

### Dig Deeper

Watch a classic movie and lay out the plot using the five stages of the stair step figure.

### Practice

Read the story of Moses in the bulrushes slowly—Exodus 2:1–10. Draw the stair step model and indicate which verses belong to each stage.

---

to the ancient Hebrews just as modern Americans are familiar with a showdown between the sheriff and the bad guys in a Western movie. *Art of Biblical Narrative*, 47–62.

3

## Character and Characterization

<blockquote>
No story has power, nor will it last, unless we feel in ourselves that it is true and true of us.... . If the story is not about the hearer, he won't listen... . A great and lasting story is about everyone, or it will not last. The strange and foreign isn't interesting, only the deeply personal and familiar.[1]
</blockquote>

John Steinbeck, East of Eden

THE TERM "CHARACTER" MEANS a person in the story such as Moses, Miriam, Aaron, David, Jonathan, Saul, Ananias, and Sapphira. The concept encompasses their physical, emotional, social, and spiritual make up. Characters are the dramatis personae (actors) who perform the actions of the plot.

The term "characterization" refers to the set of techniques authors use to depict the actors. Skillful storytellers form characters from the dust of the ground and breathe life into them. This does not imply that biblical characters are fictional; rather, it indicates that authors must be selective in choosing what to include and what to leave out. No author can say everything about every character, whether fictional or historical. Rather than trying to say everything, an author's goal is more modest: to help readers recreate characters in their imaginations and to respond to the meaning of the story as conveyed through the characters. As Culpepper states,

---

1 John Steinbeck, *East of Eden* (Viking, 1952), 239.

the biblical narrators use selection and other techniques to make "a living person live on paper."[2]

One way to understand characters is by categorizing them as "round" or flat." This concept comes from E. M. Forster in his classic *Aspects of the Novel* and has been picked up by many theorists.[3] Resseguie defines a round character as "three-dimensional, possessing several complex traits."[4] Such a character is lifelike and often unpredictable, developing over the course of the story. A round character cannot be summed up in a single phrase. Abraham, Moses, Joseph, and David are round. As you might expect, "flat" characters are one-dimensional and *can* be summed up easily. Major characters generally are round, but an exception might be the Pharisees in the Gospels. They function as major characters but can be summed up simply as duplicitous and malicious, while a minor character such as the Syrophoenician woman can be fairly round and surprise us.[5] The simple two-part system—round and flat—is probably not subtle enough to categorize many characters of the Bible, so in our exegesis we might place characters along a continuum from flat, to partial, to round.[6]

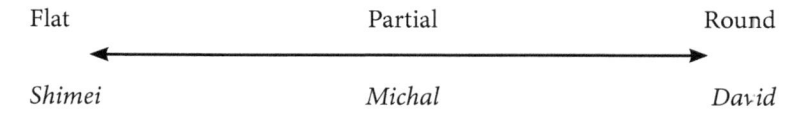

| Flat | Partial | Round |
|---|---|---|
| *Shimei* | *Michal* | *David* |

*Figure 3.1: Round and Flat Characters, a Sliding Scale*

---

2  R. Alan Culpepper, *Anatomy of the Fourth Gospel: A Study in Literary Design* (Fortress, 1983), 105.

3  E. M. Forster, *Aspects of the Novel* (1927; repr., Penguin, 1974), 75–85.

4  James L. Resseguie, *Narrative Criticism of the New Testament: An Introduction* (Baker, 2005), 123.

5  Resseguie, *Narrative Criticism,* 123.

6  Other theorists use their own categories for describing characters' functions and the degree of complexity with which they are drawn. Many of these taxonomies work from Forster's "round" and "flat" categories. For example, Resseguie subdivides flat characters into "stocks," "foils," and "walk-ons," such as the soldiers who simply do Pilate's bidding; *Narrative Criticism,* 123–123. Adele Berlin has "full-fledged" (round), "types" (flat), and "functionaries" who have little or no characterization but simply fulfill a function in the plot, such as Barabbas; *Poetics and Interpretation of Biblical Narrative* (Almond, 1983), 23–42.

As implied in my comment about the Pharisees, groups can have a collective personality and function as a single character. In Exodus, Moses constantly wrestles with "Israel," "the people of Israel," or simply "the people." In the Gospels, group-characters may include "the disciples" who are consistently thick-skulled about the mission of Messiah, and the Pharisees as noted above. Darr argues that in Luke-Acts "the Pharisees become caricatures of a morality to be avoided, for it blinds and deafens one to God."[7]

Because biblical narrative is laconic, and because it "shows" more than it "tells," interpretation of character cannot be done with scientific certainty. For example, what motivated Joseph to tattle on his brothers (Gen 37:2)? Was he being a loyal son, or was he looking out for number one, trying to puff himself by deflating the competition? Perhaps both. In any case, my point is that we cannot know with certainty why Joseph "brought a bad report about [his brothers] to his father."

Yet all is not lost. Biblical narrators do not leave readers adrift in a sea of ambiguity. Alter proposes a "scale of means" that helps us identify characters' motives, attitudes, and moral nature, and thus how certain we can be in our interpretations of those characters.[8]

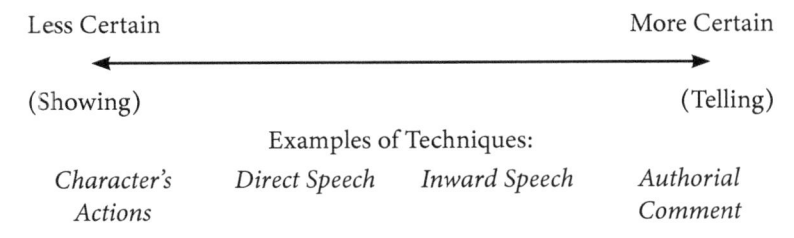

Less Certain                                      More Certain

(Showing)                                           (Telling)

Examples of Techniques:

*Character's*     *Direct Speech*   *Inward Speech*      *Authorial*
*Actions*                                            *Comment*

*Figure 3.2: Robert Alter's "Scale of Means"*

At the left of the scale we are largely in the realm of inference. The techniques used here are sometimes called "indirect presentation": "the author simply presents the characters talking and acting and leaves the reader to infer their motives and dispositions."[9] For

7 John A. Darr, *On Character Building: The Reader and Rhetoric in Luke-Acts* (Westminster/John Knox, 1992), 92.

8 Robert Alter, *The Art of Biblical Narrative* (Basic, 1981), 116–117.

9 M. H. Abrams, *A Glossary of Literary Terms*, 7th ed. (Harcourt Brace,

example, Abram gave Lot first choice of where to graze his herds (Gen 13:2–9). What motivated Abram to do that? Without being adamant in my conclusion, I would argue that the author is *showing* us the patriarch's humility in deferring to a younger man, his nephew. Perhaps his action also shows a growing trust in Yahweh who will supply all his needs. But I do not offer this interpretation as iron-clad. Perhaps Abram was conflict-avoidant and was willing to give up his rights just to keep the peace.

The middle of the scale gives us the "realm of relative certainty about character" and can be illustrated by Lot's choice.[10] You will remember that he selected lands with plenty of water. The author peers into Lot's heart to hint at his motives: "Lot lifted his eyes and saw that the Jordan Valley was well watered everywhere like the garden of the Lord, like the land of Egypt... . This was before the Lord destroyed Sodom and Gomorrah... . Lot settled among the cities of the valley and moved his tent as far as Sodom. Now the men of Sodom were wicked, great sinners against the Lord" (Gen 13:10–13). With the skill of surgeon implanting a stent, the author inserts an ironic perspective to reveal Lot's spiritual blindness: Lot looked only on outward appearances and material prosperity. He saw only the lush valley. It looked to him like the Garden of Eden. He volunteers to put down roots in a place like Egypt, Israel's paradigmatic oppressor. How ironic!

At the far end of the scale, also called "direct presentation," we have certainty in understanding motive and moral appraisal. For instance, Judas "said this not because he cared about the poor, but because he was a thief" (John 12:6); "the thing that David had done displeased the Lord" (2 Sam 11:27); when Jesus walked on water, the disciples "were utterly astounded, for they did not understand about the loaves, but their hearts were hardened" (Mark 6:51–52).

The next section continues this discussion of characterization. I have arranged the techniques from the high end of the scale to the low end.

---

1999), s.v. "Character and Characterization."

10 Alter, *Art of Biblical Narrative*, 117.

## Techniques Biblical Narrators
## Use for Characterization

### Authorial Comment

This is "direct presentation," referred to in the section above. In addition to those examples, others include:

- "Jacob loved Rachel" (Gen 29:18). This sheds light on why he labored to for so many years to win the right to marry her. It also clarifies the strained and dysfunctional relations between Rachel and Leah.
- "David was angry because the Lord had burst forth against Uzzah…. And David was afraid of the Lord that day" (2 Sam 6:8–9).
- Pilate "knew that it was out of envy that [the Council] had delivered him up" (Matt 27:18).

Sometimes prophets, angels, or other reliable characters make observations that are as certain as the words of an omniscient narrator. For example, Peter asked Sapphira, "How is it that you have agreed together to test the Spirit of the Lord" (Acts 5:9)? This provides a reliable perspective on Sapphira's deception. An ironic example is the evil spirit in the land of the Gerasenes. Having knowledge of the spiritual world which is hidden from the townspeople, the spirit calls Jesus the "Son of the Most High God" (Mark 5:7).

### Interior Monologue

As omniscient narrators, biblical authors sometimes peer into the thought processes of characters. The incident described above—Lot's choice of well-watered lands—illustrates this. The author lets the reader know how Lot perceived the options. An even clearer example is 1 Samuel 27:1, "Then David said in his heart, 'Now I shall perish one day by the hand of Saul. There is nothing better for me than that I should escape to the land of the Philistines. Then Saul will despair of seeking me any longer … and I shall escape out of his hand.'" This reveals why David took the shocking step of allying himself with Israel's enemy, the Philistines.

### Overt Speech

A remarkable portion of biblical narrative is dialogue. Perhaps fifty percent of most scenes is composed of one character speaking to another. Biblical narrators seem to trust the spoken word to carry the freight of what they want to convey. Alter observes that the Bible assumes "that what is significant about character ... can be manifested almost entirely in the character's speech."[11] Words flow from the heart and help us grasp the motives and morality of characters like Adam who blames his wife for his sin, Saul who blames the people for his disobedience, Aaron who blames the people for making the golden calf, and Jonah who blames God for his own anger. With insight, Alter states: "The Hebrew tendency to transpose what is preverbal or nonverbal into speech is finally a technique for getting at the essence of things, for obtruding their substratum."[12]

### Action

Just as dialogue in biblical narrative is laconic, carefully chosen to reveal the heart, so are descriptions of characters' actions. Unlike modern authors, the storytellers of the Bible do not describe action for sheer mimetic pleasure, such as a character stretching lazily with arms overhead. When the Bible describes actions, such as Jacob crossing his hands when blessing Joseph's two sons (Gen 48), the action is "fraught with significance."[13] Examples of characterization by describing the actors' actions can be found on every page of biblical narrative:

- Lot chooses to settle in Sodom (Gen 13).
- David dances before the Lord (2 Sam 6:5).

---

11 Ibid., 70.
12 Ibid.
13 Ibid., 80.

- A sinful woman anoints Jesus' feet and wipes them with her hair (Luke 7:36–50).
- A widow gives all she has (Mark 12:41–44).
- Disciples abandon Jesus because of his difficult words (John 6:66).
- Judas betrays with a kiss of peace (Matt 26:49).
- Jesus eats with tax collectors and sinners (Luke 15:1–2).

Action might be ambiguous in revealing the interior life of a character, but when action is clarified by what the character says, we are relatively certain that we understand the interior person. For instance, in one of those marvelous strings of verbs, the narrator describes David's actions when he received word that his child had died. He "arose," "washed," "anointed himself," "changed his clothes," "went to the house of the Lord," "worshiped," "went" home, "asked" his servants for food, and "ate." But like the servants, we wonder what this means. How has he recovered so quickly from the tragedy? David's words tell us: "Why should I fast? Can I bring him back again? I shall go to him, but he will not return to me" (2 Sam 12:20–23).[14]

## Foils

In literature, this term means a deliberate contrast. Sometimes authors set characters next to each other to highlight their qualities like placing a diamond on a dark velvet cloth. Lot is foil to Abram. The younger man is worldly, presumptuous, and spiritually blind, the opposite of the older man. The author of 1 Samuel contrasts Saul with his son Jonathan (chapters 14–15, 18–20). The father acts rashly, lacks faith, and disobeys. The son is godly, faithful, selfless, and loyal as a true king should be.

## Names

Modern readers need to remember that names in the ancient

---

14 A similar string of twelve verbs depicts Rebekah as a person of "rapid, bustling activity"; Alter, *Art of Biblical Narrative*, 54.

world (and in many cultures of the contemporary world) bristled with significance. Jesus renames Simon "Rocky," God renames Jacob the deceiver "Israel"—"Prince of God." Nabal means "fool" (his parents were prescient in choosing that name!) Abram, "Father," becomes Abraham, "Father of many nations," and he bears a son named "Laughter." In their laconic art, biblical narrators do not always name the characters—sometimes they are simply called "a widow," a "rich young man," or a "serving-girl"—so when the characters *are* named, exegetes sit up and pay attention.

The same is true of nicknames.[15] The "disciple whom Jesus loved" is anonymous, but the nickname suggests that he represents an insider's ideal point of view. Joseph is called "Son of Encouragement," and we are to see his actions through that filter (Acts 4:36). In case we missed the fact that Satan is evil, the enemy of God and humanity, the author of Revelation uses five sobriquets: "the great dragon ... that ancient serpent, who is called the devil and Satan, the deceiver of the whole world" (Rev 12:9).

### Titles, Position in Society

Once again, modern readers need to put on their ancient-narrative spectacles to read well. In the Bible, society was stratified. People understood themselves in terms of their relationships with family and power structures. In such a culture, brief phrases reveal much about characters. Ruth is called a "Moabite" (1:4, 2:6, 2:21, 4:5), a designation that portends that that she will walk a rocky road in Israel, yet a name that also displays wide God's grace as he includes a "pagan" in his plan of redemption. In the case of Naaman, the narrator labels him as both "a leper" and the "commander of the army of the king of Syria, ... a mighty man of valor" (2 Kgs 5:1). Both are true, and the descriptions reveal a somewhat round character who surprises us.

### Physical Description

In an art form marked by terseness, this aspect of biblical narrative

---

15 Resseguie, *Narrative Criticism*, 129.

may be the most laconic of all. The Bible is remarkably uninterested in what characters look like. Yet, filigrees of description occasionally ornament characterization. Absalom has long, thick hair—a mark of strength and virility which adds to his popularity. Ehud the crafty man is a lefty. The book of Mark contains virtually no physical descriptions except three portrayals of characters' clothing: John the Baptist's rugged outfit shows that he was an outsider to genteel Jerusalem, a rough-and-tumble man of God in the mold of Elijah. At the transfiguration, Jesus's clothing shone like the sun. The author shows unmistakably the glory of Jesus unveiled. And the mysterious young man in the Garden of Gethsemane fled naked.

Some minor characters in the Gospels and Acts are marked by how long they were sick. This serves the author's theological intentions, showing how the power of God can overcome even long-term illnesses: bleeding for twelve years (Mark 5:25), bent over for eighteen years (Luke 13:11), bedridden for eight years (Acts 9:33), blind from birth (John 9:1), and lame from his mother's womb (Acts 3:2). Omniscient narrators know such things, and at times they select details of physical description to contribute to the story.

By my estimate, the most fulsome physical description of any character in the Bible is of Goliath, 1 Samuel 17:4–7; yet even this anomaly is only four verses in length. The author takes special pains to show that Goliath was a biological and technological terror. Ruddy David with no armor and only a sling is no match, yet with "the name of Lord of hosts, the God of the armies of Israel" (17:45), victory comes as quickly as a fastball that ends the World Series.

Part Two of this book will discuss how to preach narratives, but even at this stage you are probably already considering how to bring the characters alive in your sermons. Try vivid language ("Goliath *bellowed*"), visual aids ("Goliath was this tall" [place a piece of tape on the wall]), use modern examples ("Goliath was bigger than Shaquille O'Neal"), and analogies ("Goliath was like a Sherman tank").

When preaching from narrative, biblical preachers are

interested in literary techniques of characterization, but our interest is not satisfied simply with increased knowledge or even aesthetic appreciation. We go on to ask the "so what" question. That is, we ask what rhetorical effects attend the literary form so that we can produce similar effects in our sermons. That's what this book is about, and with that reminder in place, we turn now to rhetoric.

## The Rhetoric of Characterization

Before a communicator attempts to change beliefs, attitudes, or behaviors, he or she must first secure the attention of the audience, and the depiction of characters in a story helps them do that.

### Attention

People are interested in people. That fact accounts for much of the popularity of interview programs on television and podcasts, as well as magazines like *People*. Preachers know the attention-getting power of stories because they have experienced glazed, wandering eyes suddenly focus when they say, "In the recent Olympic games, one member of the volleyball team from Brazil injured her wrist. But she kept playing... ." Or, "When I was 8 years old my family went on a grand road trip. We visited twenty-five states in thirty-five days. My brother and I were in the back seat of the car... ."

Narrative preachers who have done literary exegesis are well-positioned to secure and hold the listeners' attention by describing the characters in the story—their actions, words, motives, and appearance. Absalom, that handsome man, impressed the people of Israel by riding in a chariot with fifty men to run before him. He also charmed the people with flattery. He positioned himself beside the gates of the city and if anyone tried to pay homage to him, he would stop them midstream, take them by the hand and give them the kiss of peace. He feigned interest in the little problems of the little people: "From what city are you? What's on your mind? Hmm, that is a sad case, my brother. I wish I could judge your case, but, oh well ... David is busy ..." thus Absalom stole the hearts of the men of Israel (see 2 Sam 15:1–6). That is interesting! Characterization coupled with plot conflict can lift heads and focus eyes. Part Two will continue the discussion of how preachers can leverage "the predilection of people to be interested in people."[16]

One of the reasons we are interested in characters is because of "gaps." These are empty spaces, lacunae, of characterization that the listener's mind must fill in. The figure below shows a circle that is not really a circle, yet we make it a circle in our minds.

*Figure 3.3: A "Circle"*

In the example about Absalom, a relatively fulsome display of characterization by biblical standards, the author actually says very little about the *dramatis persona*. Absalom (whose ironic name means "son of peace") secured a chariot and horses, and the listener responds: "OK ... what does that mean? What is the author showing us?" Absalom positioned himself at the gates of the city, and the listener asks, "OK, why did he do that?" Absalom offered his hand to the commoners and kissed them; in her mind the listener might complete the circle: "OK, I suppose he used this nonverbal communication to flatter the commoners so he could use them in his plot against David." Through gaps in the details of plot and "in the creation of characters [an author] invites readers to 'get involved.'"[17] Authors depend on readers to be knowledgeable about the significance of things like reaching out one's hand and kissing a commoner. If you are preaching in a culture where

---

16  Culpepper, *Anatomy of the Fourth Gospel*, 101.

17  Jeanine K. Brown, *The Gospels as Stories: A Narrative Approach to Matthew, Mark, Luke, and John* (Baker, 2020), 77.

men to do not greet one another with a kiss, the gap might remain a gap unless you explain the cultural practice. Another gap might remain if modern listeners do not know that the social structure of ancient Israel was high on the "power distance" scale. That means that people expected a great gulf between royalty and the common people, and they were comfortable with that. So, when the king's son deigned to touch a mere farmer or shop keeper, call him "brother," kiss him, and give him undivided attention, it was no wonder that he won their hearts.

In reflecting on the laconic art of characterization in the Bible, Petri Merenlahti asks, "How does so much come out of so little? How do figures who are sketched with only a few harsh strokes manage to give an impression of individuality and personhood?"[18] The answer, as Merenlahti knows, is that the narrators select the most important "strokes," and depend on readers to fill in the gaps.

They do that with physical description of characters also. A "few harsh strokes" can go a long way to prompt listeners to see in the mind's eye pretty-boy David running toward Goliath like an arrow off the string; and young, well-built Joseph scrambling to escape Potiphar's wife.

## Identification

Once attention is secured, the ground is plowed for persuaders to sow their seeds, and in narrative-persuasion, sowing is done primarily with identification. As John Steinbeck says in *East of Eden* (see the epigraph to this chapter) the story must be about *us*. Even if the story takes place in a culture where farming was done with animal-power, funeral lamentation was loud and long, wedding feasts lasted for days, or Israelites despised Moabites, the story must be timeless to speak across time. We saw that in the first chapter, when I stated that art has a universal quality. The great literary critic Northrop Frye put it this way: "The poet's job is not to tell you what happened, but what happens: not what did

---

18 Petri Merenlahti, *Poetics for the Gospels? Rethinking Narrative Criticism* (T & T Clark, 2002), 77; quoted in Brown, *The Gospels as Stories,* 77.

take place, but the kind of thing that always does take place. He gives you the typical, recurring, or what Aristotle calls universal event... . You wouldn't go to *Macbeth* to learn about the history of Scotland—you go to it to learn what a man feels like after he's gained a kingdom and lost his soul."[19] In a similar vein, Frank Kermode says that "all narrative ... possesses ... some quality of parable."[20]

To move readers to adopt godly beliefs, values, and actions, biblical narrators draw us in to identify with the quirks and foibles, victories and defeats, motives and machinations of characters like Moses, Miriam, Martha, and Mary. Identification is part of authorial intention when they choose to persuade with the genre of narrative.

Rhoads, Dewey, and Michie show how this works in the book of Mark. As artist-theologian-historian-rhetorician, Mark draws a complex portrait of the disciples that causes readers to have mixed feelings towards them.[21] Like the disciples, the readers may feel honored at being called by Jesus but also frightened by the prophecy of death by crucifixion. The ones who have left all to follow Jesus cannot keep their eyes open in the Garden; they fear the storm and the one who calmed the storm; they can't seem to get it through their thick skulls that the Messiah must suffer and die. Rhoads, Dewey, and Michie state that "if the disciples can fail again and again and Jesus still promises to go ahead of them, the reader can do the same. The thrust of this portrayal poses questions for the readers: 'What will you do when faced with death for Jesus and the good news? Can you remain faithful? And can you, if you fail, begin again?'"[22]

Let's conclude this chapter by looking at characterization in the story of Jesus and Zacchaeus.

---

19 Northrop Frye, *The Educated Imagination* (Indiana University Press, 1964), 63–64.

20 "Interpretive Continuities and the New Testament," *Raritan* (Spring, 1982): 36; quoted in Leland Ryken, *How to Read the Bible as Literature* (Zondervan, 1984), 78.

21 David Rhoads, Joanna Dewey, and Donald Michie, *Mark as Story: An Introduction to the Narrative of a Gospel*, 2nd ed. (Fortress, 1999), 128–129.

22 Rhoads, Dewy, and Michie, *Mark as Story*, 129.

## Characterization in Luke 19:1–10

The three characters in this pericope are Jesus, the protagonist who is first and last to speak; the crowd, who play the role of antagonist; and Zacchaeus, the potential antagonist turned disciple. For the sake of space, I will analyze just the characterization of Zacchaeus. As deftly as a watercolorist creating a painting with a few strokes, Luke presents Zacchaeus as more round than flat, a character that develops and surprises us in just 10 short verses.

### Physical Description

Zacchaeus is short (v. 3, Gk. *tē hēlikia mikros*). That is all that we know about what he looked like, but we can infer that he was fit enough to run and climb a tree (v. 4). Being "small of stature" contributes to the plot as one of the small complications—a "stair step"—because he wants to see Jesus but cannot see over the crowd. Furthermore, shortness in the ancient world was associated with small-mindedness. When the one-word description of Zacchaeus's stature is coupled with other descriptors—"chief tax collector" and "rich"—Parsons argues that Luke the watercolorist paints this character as traitorous and greedy.[23] That is how Luke introduces the wee little man, but we see a reversal by the end of the story where he repents and becomes a true son of Abraham.

### Names

Unlike the foil to this character, the "rich ruler" of Luke 18:13–25, Zacchaeus is named. Why? Conclusions should be held tentatively, but perhaps Luke chooses to reveal his name because it comes from the Hebrew for "pure" or "righteous." Thus, Luke adds a stroke of beautiful irony—the chief tax collector is called "righteous one." That is like calling the town drunk "sobriety" or the town prostitute "chastity." But once again, by the end of the story, we see that Zacchaeus's name is a kind of prophecy because Jesus

---

23  Mikeal C. Parsons, "'Short in Stature': Luke's Physical Description of Zacchaeus," *New Testament Studies* 47/1 (2001): 50–57.

makes him a righteous one by accepting him and prompting him to repent.

### Titles and Position in Society

Three terms summarize Zacchaeus' position in society. First, he was a "chief tax collector" (v. 2, Gk. *architelōnēs*). This is the only time that the word is used in the Bible, although *telōnēs*—a subordinate tax collector—is used ten times in Luke and multiple times in Matthew and Mark. With one term, which we translate with three words, Luke tells us much. An *architelōnēs* was a district manager, who oversaw the work of subordinates in their unsavory occupation.

At this time in history, the job of *architelōnēs* was granted to the highest bidder. That person contracted with the Roman government to collect and pass on a certain amount of money, and anything the collector could grab above that amount was pocketed. Extortion and gouging were "legal," and taking bribes to allow people to avoid taxes was common. The Romans had taxes for everything—real estate, a poll tax (a flat fee per head), exports and imports at seaports and city gates, crops, wine, fruit, oil, income, use of a road, entering certain towns, animals, vehicles, sales, slaves, the transfer of property, and even an emergency tax.

An *architelōnēs* would have been unclean according to Jewish law because he had regular contact with gentiles, handled their money, and probably worked on the Sabbath because the Romans did not observe that holy day. The chief tax collector often came from outside the province or region so it is possible that Zacchaeus was not only a despised collaborator, but also an outsider. For personal profit, it is likely that Zacchaeus betrayed his own people like Benedict Arnold in the American Revolution or Quisling in Norway during WWII.

The second term applied to Zacchaeus is "rich" (v. 2). I will say more about setting in the next chapter, but if you were an *architelōnēs* in the wealthy city of Jericho, you were indeed "rich" (v. 2). In the context of the book of Luke, riches raise a tall obstacle to discipleship, but Zacchaeus is an exception to the rule, and this makes the reader marvel at the wide grace of God.

| Luke 6:24 | "Woe to you who are rich, for you have received your consolation." |
|---|---|
| Luke 12:16–21 | The parable of the rich fool. |
| Luke 16:19–31 | The parable of the rich man and Lazarus. |
| Luke 18:18–25 | The story of the rich ruler who would not follow Jesus because "he was extremely rich." |
| Luke 19:1–10 | Zacchaeus. |

*Figure 3.4: The "Rich" in Luke*

The third term is "sinner" (v. 7). This term is not the narrator's assessment of Zacchaeus but comes from the mouths of the grumbling crowd. However, in this case, the designation seems accurate. Jesus does not dispute it. Rather, he disputes the crowd's attitude toward sinners. The Pharisees also had that attitude as they link "tax collectors and sinners" in Luke 5:30 (cf. 7:34), and in that encounter Jesus provides the same response he offers in this story: "I have not come to call the righteous but sinners to repentance" (5:32).

## Action

This ten-verse pericope quotes no inner monologue from Zacchaeus or any of the actors; nevertheless, the narrator presents a round character by showing his actions. Early in the story we see the first action: "he was seeking to see who Jesus was" (v. 3). As the story unfolds, we learn that this seeking is not just curiosity. Consciously or unconsciously, he hoped for an encounter with Jesus. Today we would call him a "seeker." This surprises the reader because Zacchaeus was a "sinner." But the reader should not be too surprised, for the ultimate seeker is Jesus—"the Son of Man came to seek and save the lost" (v. 10). In Luke 15, readers have already heard Jesus use three parables to answer the Pharisees' criticism that he eats with sinners: the good shepherd, the woman who lost a coin, and the father who runs to reinstate his prodigal son. Accordingly, the reader understands that Zacchaeus seeks Jesus because Jesus seeks him.[24]

Luke subtly shows the tax collector's urgency in seeking with the next actions—he ran and climbed a tree (v. 4). These are actions for boys, not a dignified "ruler" (Gk. *archōn*) in the community. The crowd has blocked his seeking, and they will try to block it again later in the story, but Zacchaeus will not be deterred.

A gap in time may occur between verses 7 and 8. In 7 Jesus walks off with Zacchaeus to be a guest, and in 8 the repentant sinner stands to declare that he is giving half of his wealth to the poor. It is possible that between those two verses Jesus spent the night at Zacchaeus's house, and the kindness of God has led him to repentance. Verse 8 could take place in the morning as Jesus is ready to start the final leg of his journey to Jerusalem, or perhaps after a lengthy mid-day meal. One indication that a gap may occur is because verse 8 says that Zacchaeus "stood," and that word connotes more than a physical position.[25] It implies purposeful resolve and might be translated "he took his stance" as he prepared to deliver a speech intended to be overhead by the grumblers. In any case, the important thing that Luke shows is repentance, as embodied in Zacchaeus' actions and words.

### Overt Speech

Zacchaeus says little in this terse story—just one verse—but every word counts. He takes his stance and delivers this speech: "Behold, Lord, the half of my goods I give to the poor. And if I have defrauded anyone of anything, I restore it fourfold" (v. 8). These words come from a man who is being transformed by the mercy of Jesus. Romans 2:4 is apt: "God's kindness is meant to lead you to repentance." The depth of this prodigal's repentance is displayed in

---

24 Another repeated action entails words for seeing which weave in and out of the story: "behold" (v. 2), Zacchaeus "was seeking to see" (v. 3), he climbed a tree "to see him" (v. 4), Jesus "looked up" (v. 5), the crowd grumbled when they "saw" Jesus go to be the guest of a sinner (v. 7), "behold, Lord, the half of my goods I give to the poor" (v. 8).

25 Resseguie, *Narrative Criticism*, 156.

his promise to give away half of his goods. That was a lot of goods! And in Greek the statement, "If I have defrauded anyone," is a first-class conditional. This presumes (for the sake of argument) that the case is actual, and in fact chief tax collectors probably committed fraud regularly. Thus, we could translate Zacchaeus's statement, "*Since* I have defrauded ... I will repay." Zacchaeus is confessing his sin and making restitution. He promises to pay back four times the amount he swindled. The standard penalty for oppressing a neighbor was simply to repay in full, with an added twenty percent (Lev 6:5; Num 5:6–7). Zacchaeus goes far beyond that and instead obeys the law regarding sheep-stealing (Exod 22:1). The chief tax collector is admitting that he has stolen, even if gouging his fellow Jews was legal by Roman law. The words show deep heart change. Zacchaeus surprises us as he develops.

### Authorial Comment

Luke does not intrude into the plot to reveal Zacchaeus's inner thoughts or to tell the readers the "moral of the story," but the final words from Jesus serve as a commentary on the story: "The Son of Man came to seek and to save the lost." This is probably an allusion to Ezekiel 34:16, "I will seek the lost, and I will bring back the strayed." With the final words, the theology is made plain—Jesus seeks and saves wayward sinners.

Like an artist working in watercolors, Luke has sketched a quick portrait. As rhetoric, Luke's characterization has made us interested in Zacchaeus, a powerful, quirky official who runs and climbs a tree; a despised tax-collector who is called "righteous one"; a seeker who does not know he is being sought.[26] Zacchaeus is a believable character that we can identify with. His quest becomes our quest in desiring to meet Jesus in the full sense that produces life change and results in salvation. Developing a sermon from this story gives preachers an ideal text for addressing how reputation, power, and material wealth do not satisfy the heart. The story also opens the door to lift up the kindness of Jesus who stands against

---

26  See Robert C. Tannehill, "The Story of Zacchaeus as Rhetoric: Luke 19:1–10," *Semeia* 64 (1993): 201–211.

the crowd. The story is an outstanding example of Jesus fulfilling his mission to seek and save the lost.

## For Further Study

- Alter, Robert. *The Art of Biblical Narrative.* Basic Books, 1981.
- Brown, Jeanine K. *The Gospels as Stories: A Narrative Approach to Matthew, Mark, Luke, and John.* Baker, 2020.
- Culpepper, R. Alan. *Anatomy of the Fourth Gospel: A Study in Literary Design.* Fortress, 1983.
- Hunt, Steven A., D. Francois Tolmie, and Ruben Zimmerman, eds. *Character Studies in the Fourth Gospel: Narrative Approaches to Seventy Figures in John.* Eerdmans, 2016.
- Resseguie, James L. *Narrative Criticism of the New Testament: An Introduction.* Baker Academic, 2005.
- Rhoads, David, Joanna Dewey, and Donald Michie. *Mark as Story: An Introduction to the Narrative of a Gospel.* 2nd ed. Fortress, 1999.

### Talk about It

Read 1 Kings 18, the story of Elijah on Mt. Carmel. Discuss the characterization of Elijah using the categories in this chapter (authorial comment, overt speech, physical description, etc.).

### Practice

Although we have not yet talked about preaching narrative, make a list of three ways you might present Elijah as courageous in a sermon. Remember to show his character as much as you tell it. For example, you might describe what he looked like as he challenged the prophets of Baal—feet planted solidly, unbroken eye contact, and a quiet, low voice resonating with authority (or perhaps a loud, stern voice).

# 4

# Setting

*Where shall I go from your Spirit?*
*Or where shall I flee from your presence?*
*... If I take the wings of the morning*
*and dwell in the uttermost parts of the sea,*
*even there your hand shall lead me,*
*and your right hand shall hold me.*
*If I say, "Surely the darkness shall cover me,*
*and the light about me be night,"*
*even the darkness is not dark to you;*
*the night is bright as the day.*

Psalm 139:7–12

THE THIRD ELEMENT OF THE GENRE is setting. Biblical storytellers consistently include the spatial and temporal context for their accounts. This is not surprising since we live in space and time, and those environmental factors both constrain and contribute to what takes place. Experience has a "narratival quality" (recall Stephen Crites's article referenced in the Introduction). Some scholars consider setting to be third in importance, following plot and character, but this does not mean that it is insignificant, especially when we remember that each generic element overlaps with the others to form a unified representation of reality.

By setting we mean the "world" where the narrative's characters act—as specific as the Garden of Gethsemane, a sycamore-fig tree, or the Gate Beautiful of the Temple; or as general as Rome, Egypt, or the wilderness. As specific as the "the third day," or as general as "sometime later." The concept of setting includes the socio-cultural backdrop, such as the hostility between Moab and Israel in the book of Ruth, or Assyria and Israel in the book of Jonah.

When we study setting, literary exegesis overlaps significantly with standard exegesis when it uses study tools such as atlases, encyclopedias, and histories. With these tools we come closer to hearing the story the way the original recipients heard it. For example, the author of Ruth says laconically that Naomi and Ruth set out from Moab to return to the land of Judah (1:7). How far was that? What kind of terrain and topography did the two widows traverse? Do any red flags rise in your mind as you read that apparently innocuous statement? The original audience supplied knowledge of setting just as a modern American would with this statement: "A young man left his parents' home in Indianapolis and went to Las Vegas." A thousand years from now exegetes will need to pull out their study tools to understand what the author intended. As another example: the disciples took Jesus with them in "the boat" to cross the Lake of Gennesaret. What kind of boat would that have been? How big was it? How equipped were fishermen in the first century to deal with a "great windstorm" (Mark 4:36–37)?

Setting may be third among equals, but studying it pays rich dividends for preachers who take the time to understand and imagine where and when the events took place. Part Two of this book will offer some suggestions on how to incorporate setting into our preaching, but for now let's simply understand how authors use this element of the genre.

## The Elements of Setting

Setting is composed of two elements—place and time. Each of these can depict not only a literal meaning, as when Twain set *Huckleberry Finn* on a raft in the meandering Mississippi; but also a symbolic or "literary" sense. The river connotes a journey, a migration from slavery to freedom, not only for the enslaved man, Jim, but also for Huck who progresses from ignorance and apathy regarding slavery to enlightenment and empathy. By using a fictional novel to illustrate how setting contributes to a story, it is worth repeating that I am not implying that the narratives of the Bible are fiction. But they are literature.

## Place—Where the Events Happen

The literal meaning of physical space is self-evident. It refers to the geographical and topographical site of the story. It also includes things like structures—Temple, palace, tomb, and cistern—as well as natural formations such as forest, cave, and ravine. Jesus was born in Bethlehem in a stable; Hannah took Samuel to Shiloh to present him to the Lord; Saul and his sons were killed on Mt. Gilboa; Ananias lived on the street called Straight; and Gideon hid in a winepress. As mentioned above, study of geography and culture helps bring the stories alive. What was a stable like in ancient Israel? How deep and wide was a winepress?

In the Bible, description of the literal place is regularly imbued with significance beyond denotative position of longitude and latitude. We saw the same dynamic in the chapter on characterization. Biblical narrators chose only a few details of physical description, but those details often have disproportionate weight of significance. When an author calls attention to the physical space, it is likely to be important. As an example, consider the prosaic statement of setting in Ruth 1:1, "A man of Bethlehem in Judah went to sojourn in the country of Moab." The statement might have sounded like this to the ancient readers: "In 1939 a Jewish man immigrated to Germany with his family." Another example can be seen in the book of Daniel with its frequent references to court life. These contribute to the conflict of the plot because Daniel remained a true Jew without compromise even while he was surrounded by the opulent, idolatrous, and Machiavellian cabals of the courtiers.

Setting will probably not be on homiletical center stage when we preach, but it can and should be a supporting actor. The use of maps, pictures, and word pictures can bring physical place alive in our sermons. In turn, this helps us convey another aspect of place: symbolic meaning. In the Bible, as in much of the world's literature, the following sites have meaning beyond simple denotation:

- **Mountains,** such as Sinai, Nebo, Carmel, the site of the transfiguration, and the site of the great commission. Scenes that take place on mountains connote closeness to God, epiphanies, and weighty utterances. Modern parlance retains this when we speak of a "mountain-top experience," or when Dr. King intoned that he had "been to the mountain." For an interesting study of setting, notice what happens in the book of Matthew on these mountains: 5:1–2, 17:1, 24:1–3, 28:16–20.
- **The sea,** such as Moses and Israel crossing the Red Sea and Jesus stilling the storm. In the Bible, the sea was a place of chaos and danger. The pagan sailors felt this as they tried to appease the gods who they assumed were after Jonah. In Mark, the herd of two thousand pigs is destroyed in the "sea" of Galilee, a fitting grave for unclean spirits and unclean animals. Rembrandt probably understood that the sea was a place of danger, turmoil, and chaos. See how he uses light and dark in *Christ in the Storm on the Sea of Galilee* to contrast the threatening sea and the divine calm.[1]
- **The desert/wilderness** symbolizes testing, purification, danger, and isolation. Hagar almost dies with Ishmael in the desert. The children of Israel grouch their way through the wilderness for forty years until they arrive at the land of milk and honey. Jesus voluntarily fasted for forty days in the wilderness, but unlike Israel he resisted the devil, who fled from him.
- **The Jordan River** connotes a threshold experience, crossing the border into the Promised Land. In the ministry of John the Baptist, the Jordan was the place of repentance and the in-breaking of the Kingdom of God.[2] Hymns and spirituals pick up the symbolism:

---

1 James L. Resseguie, *Narrative Criticism of the New Testament: An Introduction* (Baker, 2005), 97.

2 David Rhoads, Joanna Dewey, and Donald Michie, *Mark as Story: An Introduction to the Narrative of a Gospel,* 2nd ed. (Fortress, 1999), 69.

On Jordan's stormy banks I stand,
and cast a wishful eye
to Canaan's fair and happy land,
where my possessions lie. (Samuel Stennett, 1787)

In skillful narratives like the stories of the Bible, the two levels of meaning—literal and symbolic—do not contradict each other. I am not promoting untethered polyvalence. Rather, the symbolic meaning deepens the ideational elements in the story and heightens the rhetorical impact. The same holds true for the second element of setting: time.

## Time—When the Events Happened

As is true of place, the time-element of story functions on the literal and symbolic levels. The literal level adds clarity and historical grounding to narrative, as in the book of Esther.[3] The story took place in "the days of Ahasuerus" (1:1), and the Feast of Purim was instituted on the fourteenth and fifteenth days day of the month of Adar because of the victory of the Jews in Susa (9:19–22). The literal denotation of time also enhances understanding of the book of Ezra. He fasted and mourned all night before making a proclamation to Israel about their sin of intermarriage. Within three days the nation had gathered in an open square of Jerusalem where they trembled because of their sin and because of heavy rain (Ezra 10:6–9). Details like these contribute to the atmosphere of a story, as does Mark's frequent repetition of the time-oriented word, "immediately" (Gk. *euthus*). Jesus and his followers hustle along the path of discipleship with breathless energy:

> Immediately they left their nets and followed him... . Immediately he called them, and they left their father Zebedee in the boat... . Immediately on the Sabbath he entered the synagogue and was teaching... . Immediately there was in their synagogue a man with an unclean spirit... . And immediately he left the

3 Luke places historical grounding on center stage (Luke 1:1–4) as he complied an "orderly account" from eye witnesses.

synagogue and entered the house of Simon and Andrew... . And immediately they told Jesus about their mother who was sick. (Mark 1:18–29)

The time-element of setting can be as broad as an epoch, year, or season, or as narrow as the time of day. Both the season and the hour are noted in 2 Samuel 11:1–2. David should have been doing the business of kings, but "in the spring of the year, the time when kings go out to battle, ... David remained at Jerusalem. It happened, late one afternoon, when David arose from his couch... ." And you know the rest of the story.

Another instance of a narrow use of literal time can be seen in Jesus's last hours. At midnight he prayed in the Garden, in the gray hours before dawn he was hauled before the Sanhedrin, by the third hour he was crucified, from the sixth hour (about noon) through the ninth hour darkness covered the land, and then with a loud cry Jesus gave up his spirit. That evening he was laid in a borrowed grave, but when the Sabbath was over.... . And you know the rest of the story!

Sometimes biblical narrators construct sophisticated structures of simultaneous time. Movie makers do this with techniques like split screens and jump cuts, and writers have their own techniques. Instead of using the normal conjunction, "then," they may use "and" or "while." They may also draw deliberate parallels (or foils—contrasts), between two scenes. Mark's famous "sandwiches" do this as they start one event, interrupt it midstream, and then return to it (3:20–35; 5:20–43; 6:7–32; 11:12–25; 14:1–11; 14:53–72). In Mark 3:20–35 the outer and inner stories illumine one another. At first the camera shows Jesus's family standing outside. They have come to seize him because they are certain that he is out of his mind. Then camera zooms into the house for the other event that is happening simultaneously, a debate with the scribes. Then the camera swings around to show us his mother and brothers once again who have been twiddling their thumbs. Neither group—his family nor the experts in the Law—understand him. The family accuses him of madness and the Scribes of demonic control. As Kuruvilla states, "Physical or ecclesiastical proximity to

Jesus … has nothing to do with 'insidership.'"[4] Only the one who does the will of God is his brother, sister, or mother (Mark 3:35). This skillful depiction of theological intention is made possible by the way Mark uses time and space.

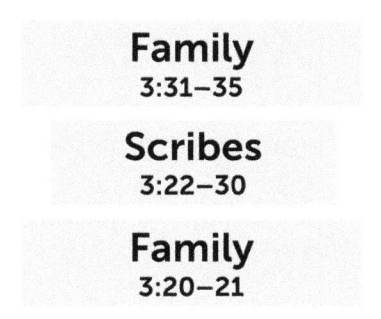

**Family**
**3:31–35**

**Scribes**
**3:22–30**

**Family**
**3:20–21**

*Figure 4.1: Simultaneous Action in a Markan Sandwich*

In addition to being literal, the time element in biblical narrative can also be symbolic. Jesus fasted for forty literal days in the wilderness, and the number forty carries connotations of Israel's forty years in the wilderness. Israel failed the tests, but Jesus passed. In the pastoral book of Ruth, the seasons of planting and harvest add delightful grace notes to the musical score. The seed comes to fruition both in the fields and in the blessed union of Boaz and Ruth. Perhaps the biblical narrator who uses time most profoundly is John, the historian-poet, with his descriptions of night and darkness. After Judas left the Upper Room to betray Jesus, the narrator comments laconically: "and it was night" (13:30). It certainly was. The plot drives steadily at what seems to be turning into a tragedy. But in 20:1, Mary arrives at the tomb while it was still dark (literally) and she was still in the dark symbolically. In the same way, Peter and the disciples fished all night and caught nothing, but then "just as day was breaking" the risen Christ appeared (21:3–6). Likewise, Nicodemus came to Jesus at night (3:1–21). John mentions this

---

4 Abraham Kuruvilla, *Mark: A Theological Commentary for Preachers* (Cascade, 2012), 71.

because the literal darkness was an apt setting to symbolize his fear and ignorance.

Including references to time and place helps authors convey character and construct plots. Thus, setting contributes to the rhetorical effects we have seen in previous chapters—things like identification with characters and building of suspense with plot. The next section of this chapter elucidates other rhetorical functions of setting.

## The Rhetoric of Setting

This generic element—third among equals—impacts readers or listeners in evocative ways.

### Imagination

A biblical author's brief comments about setting can be a catalyst that stirs the imagination. Once again, let me recommend study tools such as Bible encyclopedias and atlases to help us see the desert, the Jordan, the ramparts of Nineveh, and the hill called "the Skull." If the Lord gives you the gift of visiting the Holy Land, your imagination may get a shot of steroids. I have been there only briefly, but I will not forget one experience: our tour guide timed our travel so that we arrived at sundown at a little-used walking trail off the main highway to Jerusalem. We parked beside the road, walked the trail to an overlook, and gazed out at the Judean wilderness, just able to glimpse the northern corner of the Dead Sea. The terrain is as barren and rocky as the backside of the moon. Hawks circled above, the wind breathed softly, and the shadows stretched out cold fingers. Each person in our party found a rock to sit on, and the guide read the account of Jesus being tempted for forty days. We were looking at the actual setting, and it wasn't hard to imagine him being tested for forty days of solitude, hunger, and prayer. Forty days. Now whenever I read the account of Jesus in the wilderness, I respond more fully to the author's art and theology.

So, when the Bible describes the Temple, smell the incense. When it mentions the courtyard where the soldiers flogged Jesus, hear the sound. When it catalogues Nehemiah inspecting the walls of Jerusalem, so broken and tumbled that his donkey cannot pass, clamber over the rocks with him.

## Mood and Atmosphere

Storytellers use place and time not only to prompt us to visualize with the mind's eye, but also to tune in with the emotions. Identifying mood and atmosphere can be slippery, but they are, nevertheless, part of the author's rhetorical purpose. Literary analysis helps us grasp these components of story.

Acts 12 (Peter in prison) builds an atmosphere of danger and persecution with its depiction of guards, chains, and iron gates. Mark 5 (the demoniac) creates an atmosphere worthy of Stephen King: it takes place in the Gentile region of the Gerasenes among the tombs with a wild man who howls night and day, breaking chains like straw. In Genesis 37 (Joseph and his brothers) the atmosphere of hostility is whetted by the remote setting where the brothers plot to kill Joseph: it is a land with empty pits, barren except for infrequent caravans that trudge toward civilization, safety, and provision.

## Organization

Another function of setting is the division of long narratives into scenes. Subplots are often signaled by a change of location or time. For example, even a vague phrase like, "After these things" (Gen 22:1) can be an author's way of saying, "I'm done talking about that former incident. Now let's move on to X." The book of Acts is organized roughly by geography, as well as chronology, tracing the expansion of the gospel from Jerusalem (chapters 1–7), to Judea and Samaria (chapters 8–12), to Rome and the ends of the earth (chapters 13–29). Within those larger units, smaller stories take place in settings like the upper room in Jerusalem, the jail in Philippi, and the amphitheater in Ephesus.

The rhetorical tool of organization helps the reader track with the author so that the story has movement and coherence.

Moreover, the tool can help preachers know where to "cut" the text; that is, to know how to identify a complete unit of thought.

## Association

Biblical narrators use setting to prompt readers to make connections between the story being told and stories previously told. In particular, the stories of the New Testament reverberate with the Old Testament. New Testament scholar Jeanine Brown rightly states:

> In contemporary life, and in the Western world especially, great value is often placed on the new and the novel. Marketers know that products labeled "brand new" sell. People are constantly on the lookout for the newest fad or idea. In contrast, the Gospel writers consciously look backward; they draw from the deep well of Israel's Scriptures as they narrate the life of Jesus. They conserve as well as adapt these traditions as they interpret the arrival of the Messiah for the churches they are wanting to influence and encourage.[5]

The prompting of associations between places and events is called variously "citation," "allusion," "echoes," or "metalepsis."[6] An obvious example is the setting of Bethlehem, David's hometown, prophesied in Micah 5:2 as the birthplace of Messiah. New Testament readers would have thought of Bethlehem as the "city of David," so an association between David and Jesus bolstered Matthew's (2:1) and Luke's (2:1–7) narrative argument that Jesus is the son of David, the promised Messiah.

Exegeting echoes may strike you as speculative, or as I said above, "slippery," but the biblical authors give us warrant for the practice. For instance, Matthew reveals his own intentions in narrating the "flight to Egypt" when he cites Hosea 11:1, "Out of Egypt I have called my son." Matthew deliberately drew a parallel

---

5 Jeanine K. Brown, *The Gospels as Stories: A Narrative Approach to Matthew, Mark, Luke, and John* (Baker, 2020), 107.

6 Brown, *The Gospels as Stories,* 109.

between Israel and the Holy Family (Joseph, Mary, and Jesus). God delivered both groups by taking them to Egypt and then back to the Promised Land. Ancient people assumed continuity between the past and the present. As Snodgrass points out, New Testament authors, assumed a "reciprocal relationship between the individual and the community that existed in the Semitic mind." They also saw "correspondence in history."[7]

Thus, when Luke took the initiative to mention that God sent Peter to *Joppa* to preach the good news to the Gentiles (Acts 10), it is likely that he expected his readers to make connections to the story of Jonah. Thus, the simple statement about the coastal city morphs into a commentary rife with irony. Jonah is a foil to Peter:

Jonah went to Joppa in disobedience.... Peter went to Joppa in obedience.

At Joppa, Jonah fled from God.... At Joppa, Peter met God in a vision.

At Joppa Jonah refused to preach the message of God's boundless grace (even to gentiles!).... At Joppa, Peter [reluctantly] obeyed and preached that message to gentiles.

To conclude this chapter, let's return to the brief story of Zacchaeus to see how the setting helps the author convey his message. As with characterization, the setting of this little gem packs a lot into a few verses.

## Setting in Luke 19:1–10

From the context in Luke we know that Jesus and the disciples are headed to Jerusalem for the final time. Jerusalem was a one or two day walk from Jericho, steeply uphill. Jericho is 800 feet below sea level and Jerusalem is approximately 2500 feet above sea level. The journey by road is 18 miles through the barren wilderness I described above. The following chart takes an educated guess at the timeline.

---

7 Klyne Snodgrass, "The Use of the Old Testament in the New," in *The Right Doctrine from the Wrong Texts? Essays on the Use of the Old Testament in the New,* ed. G. K. Beale (Baker, 1994), 37–38.

| Event | Date |
|---|---|
| Entered Jericho | Perhaps Wednesday before Passion Week |
| Left Jericho (after lodging with Zacchaeus for one night). | Perhaps Thursday before Passion Week. |
| Walked to Jerusalem. | Perhaps Thursday and Friday. |
| Sabbath, probably lodged with Lazarus, Martha, and Mary in Bethany. | Sabbath rest. |
| Triumphal Entry | Palm Sunday |
| Passion Week and Resurrection | Sunday through Sunday |

*Figure 4.2: Timeline of Luke 19:1–10*

Like the tapping of a cadence leading to the gallows, Luke reminds readers that Jesus is headed to Jerusalem for flogging and crucifixion (9:21–22, 9:51, 9:57, 10:38, 13:22, 17:11, 19:1, 19:28). A pall drapes the story of Zacchaeus, and that intensifies Luke's theological message: even though Jesus was marching to his death only days away, he still had time in his "schedule" for one more stray sheep. With reverence we might say that Jesus had other things on his mind as he entered Jericho, but then the story shows us that he had the same thing on his mind that he always had: extending kindness to sinners to bring them back into the fold. Truly, he came to seek and save the lost. The significance of this timeline, even if it may be off by a day or two, is that it adds to the atmosphere and theology of the story.

Situated north and west of the Dead Sea, Jericho is warm year-round. The rich people of Jerusalem would go there in the winter because Jerusalem can be cold and damp. It was known as the "city of palms," a kind of ancient Palm Springs. Herod built his winter palace there with reflecting pools and fifty niches in the walls for statues. He also built a hippodrome and theater and placed strong fortresses on each corner of the city wall. So, it was a wealthy, Hellenized city. Jericho was on major roads leading north and south and east and west. If you were an *architelōnēs* in Jericho, you were indeed "rich" (Luke 19:2). Groves of aromatic balsam trees may have perfumed the air and the sounds of the hippodrome may have echoed, but Jesus had other things on his mind. He was interested in souls, not spectacle.

Jesus may have traveled with the throngs of pilgrims that would have been making their way to Jerusalem for Passover. It was traditional in Jericho for people to come into the streets to wish the pilgrims well as they ascended to the Holy City. In our imaginations we can hear the pilgrims singing psalms of ascent, perhaps a tambourine keeping time. Jesus was quite famous by now, so mothers might have lifted their babies to be blessed. The disciples might have acted as security guards, shepherding Jesus along the crowded road. But then the Messiah stops and fixes his eyes upward into a sycamore-fig tree. With broad branches and a low trunk, convenient for climbing, it is a convenient perch for Zacchaeus above the crowd in order to see Jesus, and Jesus wastes no time in ordering him: "hurry and come down, for I must stay at your house today" (19:5).

Here the narrator-artist-theologian becomes less descriptive about setting. He does not describe Zacchaeus's house—perhaps it was a villa—and does not draw attention to the time-element of the story except to point out the urgency of "today": "Today salvation has come to this house" (19:9). Twice before Luke has punctuated his Gospel with this word to signal momentous events: "for unto you is born this day in the City of David a Savior" (2:11), and "Today this Scripture has been fulfilled in your hearing" (4:21).

As I mentioned in chapter three, there may be a gap of time between verses seven and eight. Between those two verses Jesus may have spent the night in Zacchaeus's house, and then in verse eight he may have been setting out to continue his journey. But that is speculative. What Luke does want us to concentrate on is the final speeches—one from the crowd who murmurs and criticizes Jesus for entering the house of a sinner, one from Zacchaeus who demonstrates that the kindness of God has led him to repentance, and one from Jesus who clarifies that this is why he came to earth: to seek and to save the lost. Just as the nation of Israel entered Canaan by way of Jericho, going on to conquer and take possession of the Promised Land, so does Jesus, but his way of conquering is by laying down his life. He did not come to be served, but to serve.

## For Further Study

- Powell, Mark Allan. *What Is Narrative Criticism? Fortress, 1990.*

### Talk about It

Do you agree that authors want to spark imagination with setting? What are some dangers that might attend the use of imagination?

### Dig Deeper

Compare a modern story with a biblical story in terms of how detailed the setting is. Set a nonfiction history, such as the writings of David McCollough (*The Wright Brothers* or *The Great Bridge*), against the story of David and Goliath (1 Samuel 17) to make your comparison.

### Practice

Using the information I provided about the setting of Luke 19:1–10, how might you spark imagination and create atmosphere in a sermon from that passage? Write a paragraph or two that shows the wealth of Jericho, the somberness of Jesus headed to Jerusalem, and Zacchaeus embarrassed but desperate up in the tree.

# 5

# Point of View

*To tell a story is to create a world, adopt an attitude, suggest a behavior.*[1]

John Shea

*The author can choose his disguises, [but] he can never choose to disappear.*[2]

Wayne Booth

WHEN WE READ A STORY, we see the world through the author's eyes and we align our sensibilities, even if only briefly, with the moral universe portrayed. We respond to the author's "point of view," the fourth and final generic element of narrative that this book covers. Point of view is not as distinct of a category as the previous three elements—plot character, and setting—because it is embedded within those elements, pervading nearly all of the techniques authors use to tell stories and accomplish their purposes.

Point of view is the perspective from which a story is narrated. It "signifies the way a story gets told."[3] It reveals what is central and peripheral to the author's purposes by dictating what the reader sees and does not see. In film, the director's use of the camera creates a literal point of view. The director may wish to raise a feeling

---

1 John Shea, *Stories of God* (Thomas More, 1978), 9.

2 Wayne C. Booth, *The Rhetoric of Fiction* (University of Chicago Press, 1961), 20.

3 M. H. Abrams, *A Glossary of Literary Terms,* 7th ed. (Harcourt Brace, 1999), s.v. "Point of View."

of awe by showing an enormous mountain, so she or he may use a slow panorama, positioning the lens (and thus the viewer) below the mountain. Or the director may show the mountain with a series of close ups and jump cuts, disorienting the viewer: where are we on the mountain? What are we looking at?

Point of view encompasses not only the angle of vision, it also conveys the author's worldview and moral appraisal of the content of the story. That is how we use the term in common parlance, as when we ask someone for her point of view on the legalization of marijuana. Rhoads, Dewey, and Michie use the term "standards of judgment" to capture this, and Resseguie and Culpepper speak of the "ideological point of view."[4] Aristotle seems to have referred to the same idea when he distinguished between plot (Gk. *mythos*) and theme (Gk. *dianoia,* also translated "thought").[5] Adele Berlin puts it this way:

> The narrator is the one who controls the story. His is the voice through whom we hear about the people and of the narrative. The narrator's point of view is the perspective through which we observe and evaluate everything connected with the story. In short, the narrator ... shape[s] and guide[s] how the reader responds to the characters and events in the story.[6]

Culpepper agrees, stating that "no narrator can be absolutely impartial; inevitably a narrator ... will prejudice the reader toward or away from certain characters, claims, or events and their implications."[7] For example, the opening lines of the book of Job guide the reader in assessing all that follows: "There was a man in the land of Uz whose name was Job, and that man was blameless and upright, one who feared God and turned away from evil" (1:1).

---

4  David Rhoads, Joanna Dewey, and Donald Michie, *Mark as Story: An Introduction to the Narrative of a Gospel,* 2nd ed. (Fortress, 1999), 44–45; James L. Resseguie, *Narrative Criticism of the New Testament: An Introduction.* (Baker, 2005), 169; R. Alan Culpepper, *Anatomy of the Fourth Gospel: A Study in Literary Design* (Fortress, 1983) 32.

5  Aristotle, *The Poetics,* 1450b.

6  Adele Berlin, *Poetics and Interpretation of Biblical Narrative* (Almond, 1983), 43.

7  Culpepper, *Anatomy of the Fourth Gospel,* 32.

Ryken provides a helpful example with the story of Naboth (1 Kgs 21:1–16).[8] The first thing that secures the reader's sympathy for Naboth is his religious conviction in refusing to sell his vineyard to Ahab and Jezebel (v. 3). He called that vineyard the "inheritance of my fathers" (vv. 3–4), and family property was a sacred trust, as spelled out in Leviticus 25. (Note in passing that biblical narratives are set within the framework of didactic instruction in the Bible. We interpret the "showing" in light of the "telling" found in the Law, prophets, and epistles.) Contrary to the reader's feelings about Naboth, Ahab elicits disdain for ignoring the Law and pouting like a child (v. 4). Queen Jezebel earns our disapprobation even more. Ryken comments:

> As readers we protest every inch of the way as she manipulates the helpless Naboth, hires perjured witnesses, cruelly engineers the stoning of an innocent man, and callously tells Ahab to take possession of the vineyard. Even if we did not have the benefit of Elijah's pronouncement of God's judgment in the verses immediately following, we would know what the gripping story means.[9]

## Techniques of Point of View

How is point of view conveyed? The following five techniques summarize how biblical narrators convey their worldview and influence readers to adopt the same.

### Selection and Arrangement of Events

As I have mentioned more than once, biblical narrators select, arrange, emphasize, deemphasize, and omit materials. Pratt gives this example:

> How many options do writers have in composing a scene of a man walking down the road? They can tell us the year, month,

---

8 Leland Ryken, *How to Read the Bible as Literature* (Zondervan, 1984), 66–67.

9 Ryken, *How to Read the Bible as Literature,* 67.

day, or hour; they can report the name of the state, town, or the road; they may choose to describe the weather, the condition of the road, the people with the man, or the people not with him. The writers may describe his physical appearance, clothing, or stride; they may focus on his purposes, thoughts, or feelings; ... these and many other choices face writers who want to compose a simple scene of a man walking down the road.[10]

Consider some biblical examples of this phenomenon: Luke includes several incidents that involve poor persons, women, and gentiles. These stories are absent from the other Gospels and help Luke convey his special emphasis that the last will be first. Again, the author of Kings wrote during the Exile to argue that Israel's sin led to deportation, while the author of Chronicles wrote after the Exile; although he covers the same material, his purpose is to demonstrate that prayer and repentance are crucial for full restoration of the post-exilic community. In the example of Elijah on Mt. Carmel that we have looked at previously, the author did not describe what Elijah, the false prophets, or the people were wearing because their attire was peripheral to his purpose of contrasting the impotence of Baal with the power of Yahweh. But the author of 1 Samuel did describe Goliath's size and armaments because doing so helped him convey the truth that God can use even a young man, a shepherd, inexperienced in war, yet filled with faith and courage, to defeat a technological and biological nightmare.

Not only do narrators select what to talk about, they also arrange the events and characters to convey theology and ethics. One frequently used technique is comparison and contrast. In Chapter 4 we talked about "foils," such as Orpah and Ruth. The first daughter-in-law turned back to her home country, but the second accompanied her mother-in-law through thick and thin. Another example is the author's juxtaposition of Judah and Joseph in Genesis 38 and 39. Before I saw what the author was doing with

---

10 Richard L. Pratt, Jr. *He Gave Us Stories: The Bible Student's Guide to Interpreting Old Testament Narratives* (Wolgemuth & Hyatt, 1990; repr., P&R, 1993), 120.

this extended foil, I was confused about why he interrupted the long story of Joseph with a clumsy insertion of an unrelated story. I felt that the plot of Joseph's story was hurtling down the road when the author decided to take a detour, but I was wrong. The juxtaposition is intentional. When preaching from this passage, we might help the audience grasp the parallel by speaking from two positions on the stage—telling Judah's story here and Joseph's story there—gradually working to the center of the stage to convey the point the author is making with the juxtaposition.

| Judah (Genesis 38) | Joseph (Genesis 39) |
| --- | --- |
| Association with Foreign Women (vv. 1–3) | Separation from Foreign Women (6b–12) |
| Sexual Immorality (vv. 12–18) | Sexual Morality (vv. 6b–12) |
| Victimizer (v. 24) | Victimized (vv. 13–20a) |
| Judgment of God (vv. 6–10) | Blessing of God (20b–23) |
| Woman Provides True Accusation (v. 25) | Woman Provides False Accusation (vv. 13–20a) |
| Confession of Sin (v. 26) | Rejection of Sin (v. 10) |

*Figure 5.1: Contrasting Parallels with Judah and Joseph*

The way an author begins and ends a story is another technique of selection and arrangement. The "law of primacy" and the "recency effect" confirm that humans tend to remember first and last things longer and better than things buried in the middle. Similarly, the "end stress" of a story—the way a story concludes—is a reliable signal of authorial intention. For example, here is how the parable of the persistent widow begins and ends (Luke 18:1–8): "And he told them a parable to the effect that they ought always to pray and not lose heart.... . When the Son of Man comes, will he find faith on earth?" The reader knows without any doubt that Jesus told this parable (and Luke selected this parable) to encourage persistent prayer. Or take an example from historical narrative once again— the story of Elijah on Mt. Carmel. Its ending makes clear that God alone is the true God—the prophets of Baal are rounded up and slaughtered at the brook Kishon.

As a case study of how narrators manage time, notice how Luke tells the story of Simon the Pharisee and the woman who anointed Jesus's feet (7:36–50).[11]

| Chronological Time | Narrated Time |
| --- | --- |
| 1. Simon invites Jesus to his house. | 1. Simon invites Jesus to his house. |
| 2. As host, Simon omits the customary amenities for his guest. | 3. A sinful woman enters, washes Jesus's feet with her tears and hair, and anoints his feet. |
| 3. A sinful woman enters, washes Jesus's feet with her tears and hair, and anoints his feet. | 4. Simon silently objects. |
| | 5. Jesus confronts Simon. |
| | 2. As host, Simon omits the customary amenities for his guest. |
| 4. Simon silently objects. | |
| 5. Jesus confronts Simon. | |
| 6. Jesus pronounces the woman forgiven. | 6. Jesus pronounces the woman forgiven. |

*Figure 5.2: Management of Time in Luke 7:36–50*

A casual reader would probably not notice how Luke manages time; nevertheless, his subtle technique heightens the point being made and its rhetorical impact. Luke is saying that true faith—the kind of faith that saves (v. 50)—is marked by gratitude, love, and devotion. The one who is forgiven much, loves much. But when religious people like Simon feel that their sins are few and slight, hardly needing forgiveness, they love little.

Related to selection and arrangement is the next technique: Narrative Time.

## Narrative Time

Biblical narrators do fantastical things with time. The figure below gives examples just from the Gospel of Mark. As Kuruvilla states, "The shackles of time are shed by means of the literary liberty

---

11 Resseguie, *Narrative Criticism of the New Testament,* 209.

exercised by the narrator—all purposefully done to accomplish his agenda."[12]

| | |
|---|---|
| • Flash forward | • Foretelling of Jesus's Passion (8:31–32, 9:31–32, 10:33–34). |
| • Flash back | • Reviewing the death of John the Baptist (6:14–29). |
| • Summary | • Condensation of Jesus of Jesus's forty days in the wilderness (1:13). |
| • Pause | • Stopping the clock to add interpretive remarks (7:3–4). |
| • Ellipsis | • Silence about the day following the crucifixion (16:1). |

*Figure 5:3: Mark's Use of Time*

"Narrative time" is the relationship between *duration* of the events in the story (as measured by clock and calendar) and *length* (as measured by lines of print). The following "story" covers four years in two lines of print:

> The American Civil War was a bloody conflict between the North and the South, and the North emerged victorious.

A summary like that—hardly a "story"—wings its way across four years and half a continent. 2 Chronicles 14:5 is similar; in just one verse, good King Asa destroys the high places of every city in Judah. Conversely, when authors provide more details—more lines of print—to describe events, characters, and settings, then narrative time slows down for the reader.

The famous story of Abraham sacrificing Isaac (Gen 22) includes some summary, as with verses 2–3 (Abraham traveled for three days), but then in the moment of highest tension time slows down as the number of words expands. The author uses six verbs in two verses to describe the action in slow motion: Abraham "built"

---

12 Abraham Kuruvilla, *A Vision for Preaching: Understanding the Heart of Pastoral Ministry* (Baker, 2015), 104.

the altar, "laid" the wood on it, "bound" his son, "laid" him on the wood, "reached" out his hand, and "took" the knife to slaughter his son. The camera zooms in to focus the audience's sight and rouse their emotions.

Compare the depiction of time in Mark, with his well-known use of *euthus* ("immediately"), to Matthew and John with their long discourses and dialogues. When the audience hears a discourse, they experience it in something close to "real time"; that is, it takes about the same amount of time to read a speech aloud as it took to make the speech in the first place. Acts blends action-packed narratives with sermons and speeches so that the tempo alternates and keeps the audience tuned in.

### Word Choice

Mark Twain observed: "The difference between the almost right word and the right word is really a large matter—'tis the difference between the lightning bug and the lightning."[13] We have seen the "lightning" of word choice in the story of Naboth: different characters call the land either "the inheritance of my fathers" or simply a "vineyard" to be turned into a "vegetable garden."

Take another example: "charcoal fire" (Gk. *anthrakia*) is used only two times in the New Testament, both in the book of John. The first instance is when Peter warmed himself in the courtyard while Jesus stood trial (18:18), and the second is after the resurrection when Jesus cooked fish on the shore of Tiberias (21:9). The first is associated with testing and failure—three times Peter denies Jesus; the second is connected to remembrance and restoration— three times Peter professes his love for Jesus. John could have omitted the fire, or the fact that it was a charcoal fire, but with the artistic inclusion of this small detail, he links the events and guides the readers. We learn that denial is not the end of the story: restoration is possible for the one who remembers and repents.

---

13 https://quoteinvestigator.com/2019/09/02/lightning. Although Twain made this statement famous, he readily acknowledged that humorist Josh Billings first made the witticism.

Skillful use of repeated words is also present in Matthew 16:22–23. When Peter rebukes Jesus for being such a downer, always talking about death, Jesus rebukes him: "Get behind me, Satan." The phrase echoes the third temptation when Jesus commands: "Be gone, Satan" (4:10). These are the only two times that Matthew uses the term "Satan." Resseguie argues that "the verbal thread suggests that the two narratives are to be read in concert. Peter plays the role of Satan when he attempts to dissuade Jesus from completing his mission of going to the cross, and like Satan, he tempts Jesus to set his mind on the things of this world and not the things of God."[14]

## Omniscience

One aspect of omniscience pertains to the narrator's spatial viewpoint. An omniscient narrator can beam in and out of the setting like a Star Trek character. We see that in the story of the woman at the well in John 4: the narrator is present at the well with Jesus and the Samaritan woman when no one else is around (vv. 5–27), then with the woman in the village (vv. 28–30), then back to the well with Jesus and the disciples (vv. 31–38), then with the Samaritans that come to Jesus (vv. 39–41), then finally with the Samaritans who speak to the woman (v. 42). The example of Peter at the charcoal fire also shows the narrator beaming in and out from the courtyard to the trial and back to the courtyard.

Omniscience also includes knowledge. An omniscient narrator is aware of things that are unknown and perhaps unknowable to the characters in the story; the narrator may even know the mind of God himself:

- "The Lord was sorry that he had made man on the earth, and it grieved him to his heart" (Gen 6:6).
- Samson's parents "did not know that it was from the Lord, for he was seeking an opportunity against the Philistines" (Judg 14:4).
- Abram "believed the Lord, and he counted it to him as righteousness" (Gen 15:6).

---

14  Resseguie, *Narrative Criticism of the New Testament,* 43.

Reflecting on such omniscience, Alter comments: "It is a dizzying epistemological trick done with narrative mirrors ... and yet the self-effacing figures who narrate the biblical tales, by a tacit convention in which no attention is paid to their limited human status, can adopt the all-knowing, unfailing perspective of God."[15]

### Irony

As a powerful technique of point of view, irony takes place when the narrator knows something that a character in the story does not. The character looks at the backside of the tapestry and sees no pattern or craftsmanship; but the narrator looks at it from the front side, seeing the omnipresent and omnipotent hand of God weaving the tale. Perhaps the most famous example of irony is Caiaphas' remark to the chief priests and Pharisees as he persuades them to execute Jesus: "'You know nothing at all. Nor do you understand that it is better for you that one man should die for the people, not that the whole nation should perish.'" In case we miss the irony, John adds, "He did not say this of his own accord, but ... he prophesied that Jesus would die for the nation" (John 11:49–52).

Nathanael is also unaware of the import of his words: "'Can anything good come out of Nazareth?'" (John 1:46). The narrator prompts the reader to respond: "Yes! At least one notable exception came from Nazareth!"

Pratt sees irony in the Tower of Babel story (Gen 11:1–9).[16] The people build a city and a tower "with its top in the heavens" (v. 4), but in the next verse, the Lord "came down to see the city and the tower." With a sad shake of the head, the narrator conveys that humans may try to flaunt their independence by building high, but even the heavens are only God's footstool and he has to come down to our highest heights.

The passion narratives in the Gospels are rightly classified as masterpieces of irony. The man who is mocked as a would-be king *is* the king; the man who appears powerless *is* powerful; the man who does not save himself saves others; and the man who is

---

15  Robert Alter, *The Art of Biblical Narrative* (Basic Books, 1981), 157.

16  Pratt, *He Gave Us Stories,* 119–120.

forsaken by God still trusts God.[17] In fact, as Powell observes, "The basic story lines of our Gospels are built upon extended ironies: the people of Israel reject their Messiah; God's own Son is accused of blasphemy by characters who are themselves blasphemers; people opposed to God serve as unwitting instruments in bringing God's will to pass. Such ironies are rooted in … the idea that God's rule comes in ways that people do not expect."[18]

Point of view is the way a story is told, the vantage point the author takes. It is the narrator's perspective, tone, attitude, and judgment on the characters and their actions. Through point of view storytellers perform rhetorical magic, influencing readers to see the world as they see it and respond to it as they wish.

## The Rhetoric of Point of View

Rhetorician Kenneth Burke was right: "A way of seeing is also a way of not seeing."[19] Through point of view authors both focus and occlude what we see. They offer a vision of God and a portrait of humanity's fallen condition. They lift up heroes and put down villains. They focus attention and move the heart. I have said this numerous times in Part One, so let me offer just a bullet point summary of the rhetoric of point of view.

| | |
|---|---|
| Creates Mood | "And it was night" (John 13:30). |
| Conveys Theology | "You meant evil against me, but God meant it for good" (Gen 50:20). |
| Prompts Readers to "Decode" Meaning | "It is better for you that one man should die for the people" (John 11:50). |
| Holds Attention | Shifts in time and place in the juxtaposition of the stories of Joseph and Judah (Gen 38–39). |

17  For a moving, fascinating, and edifying exploration of irony and theology, see D. A. Carson's sermon, "Four Ironies of the Cross," https://www.preachingtoday.com/sermons/sermons/2005/august/2364.html.

18  Mark Allan Powell, *What Is Narrative Criticism?* (Fortress, 1990), 31.

19  Kenneth Burke, *Permanence and Change*, 3rd ed. (University of California Press, 1965), 49.

| Focuses Attention | Narrative time slows with six verbs (Gen 22:9–10). |
|---|---|
| Rouses Sympathy and Aversion | Nabal, Ahab and Jezebel (1 Kgs 21:1–16). |
| Satisfies Poetic Justice | Haman meets an ignominious end (Est 7:7–10). |
| Provides Models of Godly Behavior | Paul and Silas sing at midnight (Acts 16:25). |
| Communicates Indirectly, Allowing Readers to Reach Their Own Conclusions | A centurion avers, "Surely this was the Son of God." (Matt 27:54). |

*Figure 5.4: Some of the Rhetorical Effects of Point of View*

## Point of View in Luke 19:1–10

Let's return to the story of Zacchaeus, to see point of view at work. Much of this turf was ploughed in previous chapters, so I will conclude with just a brief summary.

- The name "Zacchaeus" ("righteous one") is ironic at first, but then becomes a kind of prophecy as Jesus makes him a true son of Abraham.
- Mention of Zacchaeus's profession, *architelōnēs*, heightens interest and tension because this sinner wants to see Jesus.
- Mention of Zacchaeus's small stature heightens interest and tension because these hinder him from seeing Jesus.
- The crowd serves as foil to Jesus who extends grace to the sinner.
- Some events are omitted (such as dinner and conversation in Zacchaeus's house) and some are highlighted (such as Zacchaeus's frantic actions—running and climbing a tree).
- Mention of the city, Jericho, prompts readers to draw parallels with the story in Joshua—a story of establishing God's kingdom in the land, and a story of faith of the sinner, Rahab.
- By "showing" actions like running and climbing the tree, readers must infer what the author is "telling."

| |
|---|
| • Zacchaeus's heartfelt repentance is shown by his speech, and the reader, once again, is drawn in by the need to infer. |
| • Zacchaeus's repentance, marked by restitution, moves the reader to respond similarly. |
| • The story concludes ("end stress," the "recency effect") with Jesus's theological summary: The Son of Man came to seek and to save the lost." |
| • Luke's rhetorical goals are facilitated by including this story (the only Gospel that does so). Some of those goals are to provide assurance of historical reality (see 1:1–4), convince readers that Jesus came for outcasts, and move readers to honor the Savior for his kindness and grace. |

*Figure 5.5: Point of View in Luke 19:1-10*

In Part One we have journeyed into literary-rhetorical exegesis of biblical narrative. That journey is now ended, and we are positioned for the next stage—answering the question that drives this book: how can the sermon do what the text does?

## For Further Study

- Booth, Wayne C. Booth. *The Rhetoric of Fiction.* 2nd ed. University of Chicago Press, 1983.
- *Brown, Jeanine K. The Gospels as Stories: A Narrative Approach to Matthew, Mark, Luke, and John.* Baker, 2020.
- *Kuruvilla, Abraham. Privilege the Text: A Theological Hermeneutic for Preaching.* Moody, 2013.

### Talk about It

How do the four Gospel writers depict Jesus? What differences can you find in their point of view? What did they accomplish by taking a slightly different angle of vision?

### Dig Deeper

Watch two scenes from a movie, pausing and reviewing, to notice how the director controls point of view. If you were writing the story instead of filming it, what techniques would you use to create a similar point of view?

## Practice

In your mind, film the story of Zacchaeus. Then jot down some ways you could use words (preaching) to create a similar mental movie for the listeners.

To identify the mood of the passage that you will use for your next sermon, ask yourself: if this passage were put to music, what kind of music would it be? Fast or slow? Loud or soft? How about genre of music and instrumentation: is it classical, jazz, folk, classic rock? How can you recreate that mood in your sermon?

Part Two

# Strategies for Saying What the Text Says and Doing What the Text Does

# 6

# Introduction

> *A text takes its shape from the pattern and structure of the consciousness of the author—or community—in which it was born. To follow that form in preaching is to communicate the text in the fullness of both its cognitive ... and intuitive ... dimensions of meaning. To change the form of preaching to a form not clearly representative of the text is akin to covering the cathedral at Chartres with vinyl siding.*[1]
>
> Ronald J. Allen

SO FAR IN THIS BOOK we have considered biblical narrative's literary-rhetorical features (Chapters 1–5). We have added tools to our exegetical tool belts including a visual model of plot, techniques of characterization, how narrators use setting, and the pervasive and subtle role of point of view. I hope that I have convinced you that the stories of the Bible are laden with artistic, rhetorical, theological, and ethical properties; and I hope that you share my conviction that a sermon should not only say what a text says but also do what it does. Literary form and rhetorical impact are part of the author's intention, so, in Thomas Long's memorable metaphor, the preacher's task is not "simply throwing the text into

---

1 Ronald J. Allen, "Shaping Sermons by the Language of the Text," in *Preaching Biblically: Creating Sermons in the Shape of Scripture*, ed. Don M. Wardlaw (Westminster, 1983), 30.

an exegetical winepress, squeezing out the ideational matter, and then figuring out homiletical ways to make those ideas attractive to contemporary listeners."[2] With a different metaphor, Mike Graves compares the preacher to the conductor of a symphony.[3] The conductor's job is to interpret the symbols on the page (notes and musical markings) and bring them to life for the listener. Another metaphor is the docent in the art gallery. His or her job is to help the viewer understand and experience the power of works of art.

But the main question that led you to pick up this book is still unanswered: how? For instance, how can I create suspense as my story does? How can I prompt listeners to identify with the characters? How can I awaken imagination to temporarily inhabit the setting? How can I aim the camera called "point of view"? Part Two answers the "how" question. I present six strategies with many sub-strategies for saying what the text says and doing what the text does. The first ones deal with preparation to preach narrative; in fact, they apply to preaching from many genres. Those strategies cover exegesis, the preacher's character, language, and delivery (Chapters 7–8). Then the next set of strategies deals specifically with the form of the sermon (Chapters 9–10). As you will see, when preaching from narrative, I recommend using a narrative sermon—a sermon that re-tells the biblical story rather than distilling it into propositional points.

On the one hand, we do not want to be formal fundamentalists, slavishly copying the form of the text. But on the other hand, preaching a narrative sermon from a narrative text is a natural way to say what the text says and do what the text does. Figure 6.1 offers a quick checklist of the rhetorical effects we have seen in Part One. Genre-sensitive preaching is relatively easy to do with narrative. That is not true for the other genres in the *Preaching Biblical Literature* series, and my fellow authors in the series have my respect! For example, the psalms were sung (or chanted), so does that mean that we should sing our sermons? The sentence-proverbs in the book of Proverbs are extremely brief, typically only six words

---

2  Thomas G. Long, *Preaching and the Literary Forms of the Bible* (Fortress, 1989), 12.

3  Mike Graves, *The Sermon as Symphony: Preaching the Literary Forms of the New Testament* (Judson, 1997), 18–19.

| | |
|---|---|
| ☐ Imagination | Concrete language affects the "operations of the mind" like real experience. |
| ☐ Pathos | Multiple elements rouse emotion: suspense, conflict, atmosphere, etc. |
| ☐ Attention | People are interested in people and gripped by conflict. |
| ☐ Retention | The mind remembers images and heightened affect. |
| ☐ Comprehension | Plot organizes material in a natural way, and changes of setting signal new ideas. |
| ☐ Anticipation and fulfillment | Plot points the arrows of expectation with the power of "form." |
| ☐ Indirection | Conveys theology and ethics obliquely. |
| ☐ Identification | Listeners put themselves in the place of the characters. |
| ☐ Association | The New Testament echoes the events, characters, and settings of the Old Testament. |
| ☐ Collaboration | Multiple elements produce this such as gaps left by the narrator, irony that conveys more than one meaning, and showing instead of telling. |
| ☐ Emulation | Listeners to want to follow the example of godly characters. |

*Figure 6.1: The Rhetoric of Narrative Checklist*

in Hebrew, so does that mean that our sermons should last only ten or twenty seconds? Apocalypse is laden with symbols and bizarre images, so … you get the idea. But when the text is narrative, we find the narrative sermon to be a nimble dance partner that follows the author's lead.[4]

Narrative preaching is not difficult to master, or at least it is only as difficult as mastering propositional preaching. Of the strategies

---

4 I made this argument previously in *Preaching With Variety: How to Re-Create the Dynamics of Biblical Genres* (Kregel, 2007), 27–28.

in Part Two, numbers 5 and 6 present numerous options, with the most basic option being the third-person narrative sermon (Chapter 9). This form is closest to the biblical text and is extremely flexible. When preaching from a story, the third-person narrative should be our default form for genre-sensitive preaching.

The term "narrative sermon" is as broad as an African umbrella tree, and many animals shelter under it. As stated above, its distinguishing characteristic is that the majority of the sermon is a re-telling of the story found in the text, rather than a distillation of the story into a propositional outline. To be clear, I believe that part of our duty is to communicate propositions—we are, after all, teachers and heralds—but those offices can be well-fulfilled with narrative sermons. Stories help us integrate propositions into the experiences of life and stay with us longer than most ideational content. Coming from the perspective of neuroscience, Ernest Rossi states, "Although stories may appear imprecise and unscientific, they serve as powerful tools for the work of neural network integration at a high level."[5]

This is not to say that narrative preaching is devoid of weaknesses, although you may come away with that conclusion if you read the homiletical literature from the 1980s and 90s. For all of its strengths—such as matching the form of the text, holding attention, getting around defenses, and engaging imagination and affect—this form is not the homiletical savior.[6] Its glory—indirectness—can be its downfall. If the main idea is incognito, only the most astute listeners can identify it.

But let's not go too far too fast. Before looking at options for various forms (and the potential pitfalls), let's first cover some strategies that pertain to all forms. Chapter 7 takes up two strategies related to preparation and exegesis.

---

5 Ernest Rossi, *The Psychology of Mind-Body Healing*, quoted in Richard H. Cox, *Rewiring Your Preaching: How the Brain Processes Sermons* (IVP, 2012), 41.

6 Three excellent critiques of narrative preaching are: Bryan Chapell, "When Narrative is Not Enough" in *Using Illustrations to Preach with Power*, rev. ed. (Crossway, 2001), 177–192; Richard Lischer, "The Limits of Story," *Interpretation* 38 (1984): 26–38; and James W. Thompson, *Preaching Like Paul: Homiletical Wisdom for Today* (WJK, 2001), 1–19.

# 7

# Strategies for Preparation and Exegesis

> *The preacher is a living word about God's Word before the preacher ever says a word.*[1]
>
> Barbara Brown Taylor

> *You cannot put straight in others what is warped in yourself.*[2]
>
> Athanasius

DEEP PREACHING COMES from deep preachers. I state this tautology because at times the field of homiletics underplays the importance of character formation, spiritual depth, and emotional engagement with the text and the God of the text. As we move into "strategies" for genre-sensitive preaching, I do not want to make that mistake. Before we add tools to our homiletical tool belt, we pause to make sure our hearts are in the right place. Augustine sounds the right note:

[The preacher] should be in no doubt that any ability he has ... derives more from his devotion to prayer than his dedication to oratory; and so, by praying for himself and those he is about

---

1 Barbara Brown Taylor, "Devotional Life/Lifestyle," in *The New Interpreter's Handbook of Preaching*, ed. Paul Scott Wilson and Jana Childers (Abingdon, 2008), 227–229.

2 Athanasius, *On the Incarnation*, 3.14; quoted in Abraham Kuruvilla, *A Vision for Preaching: Understanding the Heart of Pastoral Ministry* (Baker, 2015), 177.

to address, he must become a man of prayer before becoming a man of words. As the hour of his address approaches, before he opens his thrusting lips he should lift his thirsting soul to God so that he may utter what he has drunk in and pour out what has filled him.[3]

Augustine's exhortation is especially needed in a book that emphasizes creativity and affect. We are not entertainers peddling the Word of God (2 Cor 2:17). We are preachers—narrative preachers—whose goal is to honor God, serve the listeners, and move them to greater faith and obedience.

J. Kent Edwards builds on John Stott's well-known metaphor of preaching—bridge building—with the image of "closet preaching."[4] In Stott's model, the ancient text resides on one side of a chasm, the modern world resides on the other side, and in between stands the preacher. God's Word proceeds through the character, experience, and style of the preacher as he or she incarnates the written word. Edwards extends the middle element by describing how the preacher should take the text into the private closet of prayer, meditation, and obedience. Only then will the preacher speak with sincerity and power.[5]

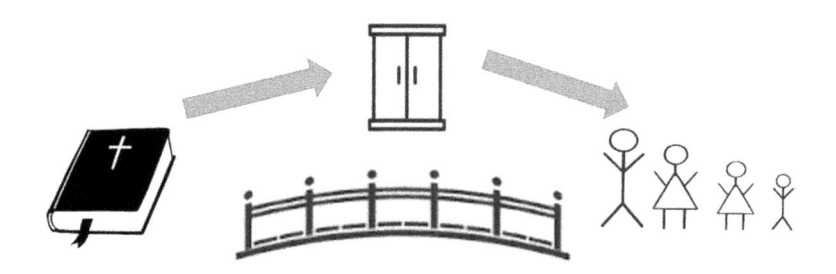

*Figure 7.1: Closet Preaching*

3 Augustine, *On Christian Teaching*, 4.32, trans. R. P. H. Green (Oxford University Press, 2008), 121.

4 J. Kent Edwards, *Deep Preaching: Crafting Sermons that Go Beyond the Superficial* (B&H, 2009).

5 See also Fred B. Craddock, *Preaching* (Abingdon, 1985), 22.

## Strategy 1: Pray

It feels funny to label this a "strategy," but I offer it as a reminder. Biblical narratives are the inspired Word of God, theologically and ethically imbued, intended for edification, so we ask God to help us interpret them rightly.

I preached my first sermon when I was sixteen, and no one had to remind me to pray! I prayed as I selected a text (not really knowing how to do so), as I studied the text (not really knowing how to do so), as I wrote the sermon (not really knowing ...), and as I walked forward to preach. Desperation is the mother of prayer.

That was probably the high point of my dependence on God in my preaching ministry. I need to get back to that. How about you? As we gain skills, knowledge, and experience we are tempted to rest on that foundation, but as valuable as those attainments are, any foundation other than Christ is sinking sand.

When should we pray? Always. "Pray without ceasing" (1 Thess 5:17). Abraham Kuruvilla calls it "habitual prayer: in the gym, as we drive, in the study, as we counsel, in the sanctuary, and as we rise each morning and retire each night. We do not want to be like the Israelites in the book of Judges who went through cycles of prosperity, then forgot God, then were oppressed by foreign powers, then finally cried out to God. The art of walking with God is keeping the cycle tight.

One of the many benefits of habitual prayer is to remind us of God's unceasing presence.[6] All is "naked and exposed to the eyes of him to whom we must give an account" (Heb 4:13). Kuruvilla illustrates this with the story of Udo Wächter, who worked at the University of Osnabrück in Germany. For six weeks in 2004 he wore a wide belt lined with thirteen vibrating pads like the ones that make a cell phone buzz. Sensors on the belt detected the earth's magnetic field and whichever buzzer was pointed north buzzed. Without ceasing. For six weeks. Wächter says he learned a lot. For example, he never realized how much roads wind around as they travel from point A to point B. Eventually, this occurred: "I suddenly realized that my perception had shifted. I had some kind of internal map of

---

6  Kuruvilla, *A Vision for Preaching*, 178–181.

the city in my head. I could always find my way home. Eventually I couldn't get lost, even in a completely new place." Wächter even felt the buzzing in his dreams, always orienting him north.[7]

That is what preachers need—an unceasing consciousness of God. Habitual prayer keeps us aware of "north."

Another kind of prayer might be called "seasonal" or "regular." This is the prayer of daily devotions and periodic retreats. Such prayer is not an exact science, and each person will find his or her own way, but this kind of prayer might include praying Scripture back to God, listening in silence, fasting, or journaling. The time-tested acronym of ACTS helps leads us through four kinds of prayer: Adoration, Confession, Thanksgiving, and Supplication. The key is not so much the form regular prayer takes but its regular practice. Prayer is like the propane that fuels the backyard grill. We may not know that the tank is empty until the heat stops.

Whether we are engaged in "habitual prayer" or "regular prayer," we should pray for our preaching and for our listeners. The Apostle Paul asked for such prayer, that he would "proclaim the mystery of the gospel ... boldly" (Eph 6:18–20).

We should also pray for illumination. While "inspiration" refers to God's finished communication collected in the canon of Scripture, "illumination" refers to God's ongoing communication as the Spirit sheds light on the inspired Word. It is needed to discern the meaning of the text and its significance.[8] Many of us need to recover the doctrine of illumination.

As we study the text, the Holy Spirit is like a tour guide on a walking tour. I love to take walking tours, and I enjoy them most when an expert points out the architecture, history, and oddities of the locale. I live near Boston, one of the great historical cities of the U. S., and while touring the posh area of Beacon Hill, the guide called our attention to some of the windows of the nineteenth-century brownstones. The windows have a purple tint. This is because of impurities in the glass—manganese oxide. When the windows were new, they were perfectly clear, but sunlight interacted with the oxide to turn them purple. The defective windows are now

---

7  Ibid., 180.

8  Robert Stein, *A Basic Guide to Interpreting the Bible* (Baker, 1994), 43.

collector's items. If I had been walking through the neighborhood on my own, I probably would have missed the fascinating windows, but the guide helped see what I was looking at. Just so, the Holy Spirit illumines us to see what we are looking at in the text. Spurgeon said, "Your prayers will be your ablest assistants while your discourses are yet upon the anvil."[9]

We pray not only about the text—its meaning and application—but we also pray for the listeners themselves. We might walk through the sanctuary and pray for the Millers who sit over there on the right and Mr. Garcia who just lost his wife. He sits over there, but you haven't seen him lately. As we walk to the back of the room, we pray for the teenagers who favor that section. Or we might pray through the church's pictorial directory. The elders in my church and I did this for years, writing quick emails to the people after we prayed for them. Doors for pastoral ministry open with that simple practice. The people often wrote back not only to say thank you, but also to inform us about the happenings of their lives. As you pray for the listeners, you might enlist a team that prays for you even as you are preaching, or who offer prayer at the close of each service.

When it comes to praying and sermonizing, the most helpful model I have found is from *The Supremacy of God in Preaching* by John Piper. Praying through these five steps helps us depend on God and not ourselves, even as we work hard on our sermons. I have adapted Piper's acronym a bit:[10]

**A**cknowledge

**P**lead

**C**laim

**A**ct

**T**hank

*Figure 7.2: How to Rely on God in Our Sermon Preparation*

---

9 C. H. Spurgeon, *Lectures to My Students* (1875; repr., Baker, 1977), 41.

10 John Piper, *The Supremacy of God in Preaching*, rev. ed. (Baker, 2004), 47–49.

- **A** stands for Acknowledge. State to God in plain terms: "Without you, my sermon will be wood, hay, and stubble. This is true, and I confess it."
- **P** stands for Plead. In light of the acknowledgment, we petition God: "Please move powerfully. Convict, comfort, remind, teach, and do whatever is required in each heart."
- **C** stands for Claim. In faith, boldly latch onto God's promise to use his Word and the preaching of his Word. I have found that my preaching text almost always contains a promise or an implication that I can claim regarding my upcoming sermon, but if not, we have plenty of promises to draw from, such as "Faith comes from hearing" (Rom 10:17), and "You have been born again … through the living and abiding word of God… . This word is the good news that was preached to you" (1 Pet 1:23–25). The Word is a lamp that illumines (Ps 119:105; Prov 6:23; 2 Pet 1:19), a hammer that breaks up stony hearts (Jer 23:29), a sword that pierces the conscience (Heb 4:12), milk that nourishes a baby (1 Pet 2:2), rain that refreshes the crops (Isa 55:10–11), and a mirror that shows us our true selves (Jas 1:23–25).
- **A** stands for Act. Study your text, analyze the audience, plan the moves, gather the illustrations—not in proud self-reliance as if the success of the sermon depends on you alone, but because God has commanded us to act. We act because we have faith in him, not ourselves.
- **T** stands for Thank. When the sermon is over, rather than rehearsing your mistakes (there were probably many), give God praise for using his word and using you. I remember John Ortberg telling the story of when he and his mentor, Dallas Willard, spoke from the same stage at a conference.[11] At the end of the evening as they walked together through the parking lot, John was doing his normal post-platform routine of worrisome self-talk: "How did I do? Did they like me? Oh, rats, I forgot that point." By contrast, Dallas was humming softly as he strolled. He was not tied up in knots. He had done his best with his lecture and had released it like a dove. Now it was in God's hands and

---

11 I am unable to find the source for this story, but I remember reading it in one of John's books or hearing it in one of his addresses. If I made it up, I hope John will forgive me!

the hands of the listeners. Peter Scazerro would say that Dallas Willard was "emotionally healthy." Scazerro explains, "If I'm too concerned about what people think of me and how the sermon is going to come off, I don't think I'm ready to preach."[12]

A prayer of thanks after preaching reminds us that through the foolishness of preaching God saves and sanctifies.

### Strategy 2: Engage Your Imagination

By "imagination" I do not mean eisegesis and flights of fancy. I mean yielding to the author's intention. If he describes Absalom suspended by his head between heaven and earth, the meditative exegete pauses to think about what that looked like and felt like. If the author describes Ruth and Boaz at the threshing floor in the gray hour before dawn, what did that feel like and sound like? Was it cool, damp, and muffled? As we have seen, narrative communicates primarily by showing rather than telling, so responsible exegesis reads slowly and imaginatively. On Mount Carmel the fire of God falls. Feel the heat. On the Mount of Transfiguration Jesus's garments shine like the sun. Shade your eyes. On Mount Sinai fire and smoke wreath the mountain. Better get a respirator!

You may have heard the baseball adage: "Go with the pitch." This means that if the pitcher pitches a ball that is outside (far from you), then the easiest way to hit it is by pushing it away from you rather than pulling it across your body. For a right-handed batter this means hitting it to right field. If the pitch is inside, close to your body, then you can pull it to left field. The point is, you have to "go with the pitch"—respond to the opportunity that is presented, yielding to the trajectory of the ball rather than resisting it. Similarly, biblical preachers need to "go with the text." Francis Bacon was not thinking of narrative preaching when he defined "rhetoric," but for our purposes he is spot on: "The duty and office of Rhetoric is to *apply Reason to Imagination* for the better moving of the will."[13]

---

12 Peter Scazzero, "The Importance of Being an Emotionally Healthy Preacher," in *Sermon Preparation*, ed. Craig Brian Larson (Hendricksen, 2012), 35.

13 Francis Bacon, "Advancement of Learning," in *Selected Writings of Francis*

Do I hear someone objecting that "imagination has no part in the science of exegesis? It allows reader-response criticism to sneak through the backdoor. Before you know it, the parlor will be spoiled with the reader's muddy boots and grubby fingerprints."

My response is twofold. First, an unbridled imagination can detour us from the author's intention. I have seen this happen in the classes I teach, and I am sure that I have engaged in imaginative eisegesis myself. (I remember as a teenager preaching on Ephesians 6, the armor of God. I pictured "God's white knight" in medieval armor, not the kit of a Roman soldier.) However, a more frequent problem is the suppression of imagination. We chop the literature of the Bible into smidgeons of data, re-form it into an exegetical McNugget, preserve it, package it, and call it exegesis.

My second response corrects both of these problems—the overreaching and underreaching imaginations: tether imagination to the text. Patricia Batten quotes John Burroughs on this subject: "To treat your facts with imagination is one thing, but to imagine your facts is another."[14] I am recommending the former while avoiding the latter. I have found that careful exegesis of standard issues like context, culture, geography, word study, and syntax provide plenty of fuel for the fire of imagination. When we add literary-rhetorical exegesis to our stock of tools, we have all we need to let the story rise. Some examples illustrate what I have in mind.

- When preaching from Acts 9 (the conversion of Saul), I begin the narrative portion this way: "Saul's muscles tensed and his heart pounded. His breathing sounded like an animal snorting and bellowing as he thought of those ... what did they call themselves? He spat out the word: 'Christians.'"

Where is this "snorting and bellowing" in the text? It is implied in 9:1, "Saul, *breathing out* threats and murder against the

---

*Bacon* (New York: 1955), 309, quoted in Golden, Berquist, and Coleman, eds., *The Rhetoric of Western Thought*, 3rd ed. (Kendall/Hunt, 1983), 127.

14  Patricia Batten, "The Story of the Worship Leader," in *Models for Biblical Preaching: Expository Sermons from the Old Testament*, ed. Haddon W. Robinson and Patricia Batten (Baker, 2014), 75.

disciples." Word study of that verb shows that it is a present participle indicating ongoing action, and the word was used in Greek literature for the growling of wild animals and the snorting of war horses. In didactic, lecturing-fashion, I could say: "The verb in verse one is used in Greek literature for... . It indicates that Saul was quite angry and upset." Or I could *show* that truth.

- In my sermon on Jesus casting out Legion (Luke 8:26–39), I describe the demon-possessed man addressing Jesus: "The words tumble and collide and interrupt each other; he can hardly put together a coherent sentence: 'What ... to me ... and to you ... Jesus?'"

How do I know that his words tumbled and collided? The syntax of the sentence in Greek is broken. Luke *shows* us the man's agitation as he hisses and spits his words.

- In a sermon on Ruth 1, I describe Naomi and Ruth lurching into Bethlehem. They are travel stained and weary, footsore and beat. The whole town is stirred, and the women speculate about who the ladies might be (1:19).

This example is a bit more speculative than the ones above, but I make it based on study of geography and culture as explained in previous chapters of this book. Bethlehem was many miles west and north of Moab. The two widows would probably have taken the road on the north side of the Dead Sea, forded the Jordan River (there were no bridges), sweated through the dense thicket of the Jordan Valley, passed through Jericho, and then climbed the steep incline to Bethlehem (which is even higher in elevation than Jerusalem). Culturally, the two destitute widows would not have had transportation except their own feet, and they probably carried no more than they could lug. Furthermore, in a small town in a collectivistic society, where fields were worked communally, everyone knew all the doings of the neighborhood.

To exegete with imagination, I recommend the following strategies.

### Strategy 2.1: Exegete with Standard Tools of Language and History

In particular, spend some time on culture and geography as with the example above about Naomi and Ruth. Study of culture helps with Acts 27 also, the vivid story of shipwreck. How large were first-century sailing vessels? How did they respond in a violent storm? Why did the sailors run ropes under the keel, and how did they do that? Knowledge of such things equips the preacher to re-tell the story with verve.

### Strategy 2.2: Read Slowly

This is one of the benefits of doing good exegesis—it causes us to slow down, a kind of "forced" meditation. Find a quiet place. Re-move the ubiquitous distractions that elbow in by buzzing, chirp-ing, dinging, and whirring.

### Strategy 2.3: Listen to the Text

The ear notices things the eye misses. A skillful reader can bring the text alive through "oral interpretation." That is the term for the field of communication studies related to reading aloud from the printed word. When we read aloud, we must make choices about the meaning and mood of the text. What did Jesus sound like when he rebuked the Pharisees? Angry, sorrowful, playful? How about when he rebuked Martha? When the sailors threw things over-board, and eventually threw Jonah overboard, were they desperate or calm, saddened or relieved to get rid of the wayward prophet?[15]

### Strategy 2.4: Try "Logosomatic" Study[16]

This is Thomas Troeger's term for "word-body." As you read the narrative, get your body involved and you will use sections of your

---

15  To listen to the text, try some of my favorite Scripture readers, easily found with an internet search: Alexander Scourby, Max McLean, David Suchet, Hunter Barnes, and Courage for Life (multiple female readers).

16  Thomas Troeger, *Imagining a Sermon* (Abingdon, 1990), 53–58.

brain that are dormant in silent, standard exegesis. If the biblical narrator says that Moses stretched out his hands, stretch out your hands. If the narrator says that the Egyptians made life miserable for the Israelites with the hard service of bricks and mortar, pick up some bricks. If the narrator says that they broke bread at the first Passover, break some bread.

### Strategy 2.5: Make a Mental Movie[17]

As with oral readers, filmmakers must make interpretive choices to *show* what they wish to emphasize. As David and his men return to Ziklag only to find that the Amalekites have "burned it with fire" and taken all the women and children (1 Sam 30:1–6), perhaps the camera in your mind begins with a long shot—smoke is rising over the ridge. As David and his raiders approach the village, perhaps you see a close-up of their faces as they realize what has happened. Then as they lift their voices to weep "until they had no more strength to weep." You get the idea.[18]

These strategies of preparation set us up to preach engaging and edifying sermons. The next batch of strategies moves even closer to our goal of doing what the text does.

### For Further Study

- Sunukjian, Donald R. "The Credibility of the Preacher." *Bibliotheca Sacra* (1982): 255–267.
- McClellan, Dave. *Preaching By Ear: Speaking God's Truth from the Inside Out.* Weaver Books, 2014.

### Talk about It

- Do you tend to overreach or underreach with your use of imagination during exegesis?

---

17 David Day, *Preaching with All You've Got: Embodying the Word* (Hendricksen, 2005), 32.

18 Actual films such as the multi-part series, *The Chosen*, can help also, but the image you make in your mind, guided by sound exegesis, is superior.

- Are most preachers Mary or Martha? That is, do they tend toward quietude or activity? How about you?

## Dig Deeper

What do these passages suggest that ministers need in terms of their personal character? Make a list.

- 1 Thessalonians 2:1–12
- Acts 20:17–35
- 1 Peter 5:1–4

## Practice

- Try two of the suggestions in this chapter to add imagination to your exegesis.
- Pray for the people who will hear your next sermon. Over time, name them one by one.

# 8

# Strategies for Presentation:
# Language and Delivery

*There are bright words, as brilliant as a tropical sunrise, and there are drab words, as unattractive as a country bus station. There are hard words that punch like a prizefighter, and weak words as insipid as tea made with one dunk of a tea bag. There are pillow words that comfort people and steel-cold words that threaten them. Some words transplant listeners at least for an instant close to the courts of God, and other words that send them to the gutter. We live by words, love by words, pray with words, curse with words, and die for words.*[1]

Haddon Robinson

*The purpose of literature is to turn blood into ink. [And the purpose of preaching] is turn the ink back into blood.*[2]

Charles Bartow

*No mortal can keep a secret. If his lips are silent, he chatters with his fingertips; betrayal oozes out of him at every pore.*[3]

Sigmund Freud

---

1 Haddon W. Robinson, *Biblical Preaching: The Development and Delivery of Expository Messages*, 3rd ed. (Baker, 2014), 136.

2 Charles L. Bartow, *The Preaching Moment: A Guide to Sermon Delivery* (1980; repr. Kendall/Hunt, 1995), 15.

3 Sigmund Freud, *Collected Papers*, vol. 3 (Basic, 1959), 94; quoted in Robinson, *Biblical Preaching*, 151.

LIKE THE FIRST two strategies, the ones in this chapter apply to all preaching, but I single them out because of their special importance for genre-sensitive preaching of narrative. Why are language and delivery so important? Because many of the rhetorical effects of the genre rise or fall with the preacher's presentation. For example, the author of Exodus wanted to stir imagination and emotion with the crossing of the Red Sea. Abstract, colorless language will turn that story into, as Robinson says above, tepid "tea made with one dunk of a tea bag"; and flat, detached delivery will stir no one. The expository preacher who wants to do what the text does acknowledges the importance of vivid language and passionate delivery. These are primary, not secondary, in reproducing the effects of the text.

## Strategy 3: Use Vivid and Clear Language

Biblical narrators spoke with concrete language, so the genre-sensitive sermon follows suit. Because the narrative preacher spends a good portion of his or her time showing rather than telling, the language must paint pictures in the mind. To do that, our descriptions will probably be more fulsome than the text's. This is because the biblical story is laconic, almost a shorthand mode of storytelling, but as we have seen, lots of color, emotion, and nuance fills the biblical package, and to bring that out in our own context we will probably need the tools described in Strategy 3.

Alison Gerber is a master storyteller, including the use of vivid language. The following passage comes from Gerber's sermon on Acts 27, the shipwreck as Paul traveled to Rome.[4] She describes the storm approaching in the distance. The sailors see it and their hearts sink:

> They see it whipping over the mountains on the coast. It lifts thickets and dumps them into the sea. They see it bend trees. Then it hovers over the ocean, whipping up the waves, and as it approaches it begins to drizzle, then pitter-patters, and then

---

4 Alison Gerber, "God Keeps His Promises," unpub. sermon, preached March 2017.

showers. And then it's bucketing down, and it's coming in sideways, and then darkness covers them in her blanket.

After fourteen days of this (fourteen days—can you imagine?), a sailor cries out, "I think I hear something. Could it be the sound of waves breaking on the shore?" They lower the line to measure the depth of the ocean, "120 feet!" They lower again, "90 feet!" The captain shouts, "We're approaching land," and the sailors say, "And we're approaching it fast." They lower anchors into the water—one, two, three, four anchors—hoping to slow the ship's progress. The whole boat rouses now, and everyone's pressing against each other, straining to hear the sound of waves on the shore: "I think I can hear it! I can hear it! I'm sure I can hear it!" And as the passengers crowd the rails, quietly, quietly, those sailors are slipping supplies into the lifeboat. They push it into the ocean. Splash! "What was that sound?!" a prisoner calls. "No nothing, just an anchor." But Paul is keeping watch: "Julius! Look there! Unless these men stay with the ship we cannot be saved!" So the soldiers do what they should have done at the beginning, they listen to Paul. They take their swords and cut the rope and let the lifeboat drift into the dark. "What are you doing?!" the sailors cry, "You would give up the real chance that some of us might be saved for the unreal dream that all will be saved? Are you, crazy?" And this is when Paul gets up and plants his feet on a little crate on the deck as the ship rolls and pitches and yaws. He says, "For the last fourteen days you have been in constant suspense, and you haven't eaten a thing. Now, I urge you to take some food, you need it to survive. Not one of you will lose a single hair on his head." And there on that little crate he breaks bread and gives thanks to God before them all.

Let's break Strategy 3 into specific techniques. You might want to keep Gerber's passage before you to see the principles in action.

## Strategy 3.1: Use Concrete Verbs and Nouns

With a genre that shows more than it tells, the preacher will want to do the same by using concrete words. Come down the "ladder of abstraction."

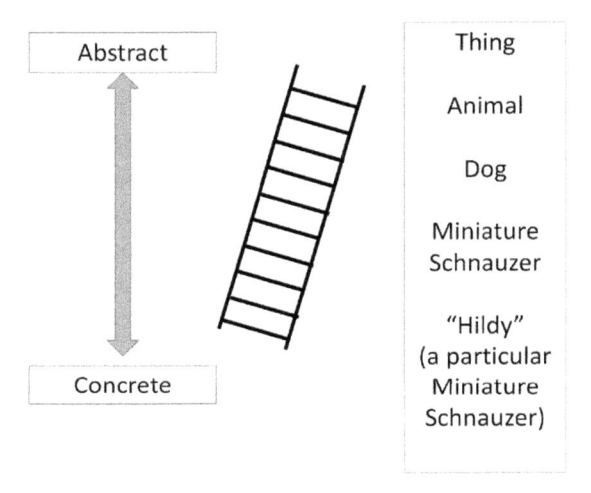

*Figure 8.1: Ladder of Abstraction*

Instead of saying, "The man *went* across the street," try "sauntered," "sprinted," "stumbled," or "skipped." Instead of "a pleasurable past time" try "knitting," "wood carving," or "singing in a barbershop quartet." The image is in the verb and noun. Adverbs and adjectives do little to dress up a vague sentence ("It truly was a really, really big thing"). Master stylist E. B. White put it this way: "The adjective hasn't been built that can pull a weak or inaccurate noun out of a tight place."[5] How might you recast these sentences so that they are lower on the ladder of abstraction? (I have done so in italics).

He showed satisfaction as he took ownership of his well-earned recompense.
*He grinned as he snatched the coin.*

There were a great number of dead leaves lying on the ground.
*Dead leaves covered the ground.*

---

5 William Strunk, Jr., and E. B. White, *The Elements of Style*, 4th ed. (Macmillan, 2000), 71.

Did you notice Gerber's concrete verbs? The approaching storm "whips," "lifts," "dumps," "bends," and "hovers." Then it "drizzles," "pitter-patters," "showers," and "buckets down."

Instead of using a static helping verb such as "Goliath's sword *was* heavy," show the same idea: "David strained to hold Goliath's sword overhead." Prompt the listeners to conclude: "Wow, that must have been a heavy sword."

One way to put pizzazz into your language is with fresh figures of speech. Metaphors and analogies can borrow from modern culture to make the ancient narrative understandable and vivid. The Syrian commander Namaan might be a "five-star general"; Goliath, a "Sherman tank"; and businesswoman Lydia might own a company called "All Things Purple." Galli and Larson describe King Jeroboam as a competent and professional manager: "Jeroboam took off his sandals and put on black wing tips."[6] Similarly, Eugene Peterson describes David's brother Shammah as "a mincing little sophisticate in Calvin Klein jeans and alligator cowboy boots."[7]

It is not necessary to become a Steinbeck or Hemingway, and developing such style would take a lifetime, overwhelming the busy pastor, so perhaps you could wordsmith just one paragraph a week in each sermon. Then, over the course of years, your style will gradually become vivid. Figure 8.2 gives more advice from Jennifer Lord to develop effective style for narrative preaching.[8]

---

- Read excellent literature.
- Read aloud.
- Write letters.
- Review your manuscripts for clichés and overused phrases.
- Play word games.
- Talk with small children.
- Pick a word and write a page about it without using the word.

---

*Figure 8.2: How to Develop Effective Style*

---

6 Mark Galli and Craig Brian Larson, *Preaching that Connects: Using Journalistic Techniques to Add Impact* (Zondervan, 1994), 82–83.

7 Quoted in Steven D. Mathewson, *The Art of Preaching Old Testament Narrative*, 2nd ed. (Baker, 2021), 153–154.

8 Jennifer L. Lord, *Finding Language and Imagery* (Fortress, 2010), 51–52.

## Strategy 3.2: Avoid Excess

In teaching narrative preaching for many years, I have noticed that my students take Strategy 3.1 to heart, but then sometimes they sound like bad poetry—bloated or saccharine. Too much description in storytelling is like too much sugar in coffee. Consider this:

> David rose from his comfortable couch, there on the roof of his palace, with soft breezes flowing around him like a silk robe. With complacency he stretched his muscular body like a lazy dog roused from a sleepy, midday nap. Upward and outward he turned his gaze to the setting sun, a ripe orange fruit set against the azure blue of the Middle Eastern sky. Slowly it sank toward the vast rim of the horizon like a weary soldier returning home from fatiguing campaigns abroad. "My, my," he thought as he remained still, "How lovely and beautiful."

Try this instead:

> David rose and stretched like a lazy dog. He was on the roof of his palace. The sun was starting to set, brilliant orange against the blue sky. "My, my; how beautiful."

## Strategy 3.3: Cut Clutter

This strategy is cousin to the previous one, but here I mean reducing the number of words, particularly useless ones. In *The Art of Plain Talk*, Rudolf Flesch contends that clarity increases proportionately as sentence length decreases.[9] Speakers who feel insecure sometimes bloat their language to sound, as they think, educated; but as Robinson quips, "A sermon is not deep because it is muddy."[10] Figure 8.3 gives examples of a clutter-free style from the classic *Elements of Style*.[11]

---

9  Rudolph Flesch, *The Art of Plain Talk* (Harper, 1946), 38–39.

10  Robinson, *Biblical Preaching*, 139.

11  Strunk and White, *Elements of Style*, 23–24. Also helpful is Galli and Larson, *Preaching that Connects*, 91–104.

| | |
|---|---|
| • He is a man who | • He |
| • This is a subject that | • This subject |
| • His story is a strange one. | • His story is strange. |
| • The fact that he had not succeeded | • His failure |
| • It was not long before he was very sorry that he had said what he said. | • He soon repented his words. |

*Figure 8.3: Cut Clutter, from Elements of Style*

I have trimmed the fat from the paragraph below by eliminating 51 of 115 words. Remember that delivery can convey much of what is cut:

Zacchaeus stared at the tree ~~for a really long time~~. Should he or shouldn't he? What would people think ~~and how would they feel about him~~? And besides that, could he? He hadn't climbed a tree since he was ~~just~~ a ~~little~~ boy. Looking ~~slowly~~ up and down ~~the length of~~ the trunk for some ~~possible~~ handholds ~~which would make the job a lot easier~~, he ~~finally~~ made up his mind ~~in virtually no time at all~~. Up he went ~~quickly~~. He wasn't used to this boyish exertion! But ~~by pushing and pulling really, really hard~~, he ~~very~~ soon ~~found himself~~ perched in the ~~many, leafy~~ branches ~~like a bird~~. And ~~then~~ here came Jesus!

To learn to cut clutter, try writing a "cinquain," a five-line poem. One form of the cinquain has two syllables in the first line, four in the second line, six and eight in lines three and four, and then back to two syllables for the final line:

Baseball:
Bats crack and smash
The pitch, propelling it
Out, over the fence, heads, and cheers.
Homerun!

### Strategy 3.4: Use Oral Language

Many rules governing good writing apply to good speaking, but some do not. Oral language tends to be less formal than written. It is comfortable with short sentences (even fragments), sound effects and onomatopoeia (buzz, bang, boom), personal pronouns (I, we, you), contractions, redundancy, and the normal syntactical breakup of speech. As an enlightening exercise, audio record a conversation and then write an exact transcript. It will be almost incoherent!

> So, the other day, uhm, yesterday I guess, I don't know, I was riding my bike to, you know, Crosby's. And you know what happened? Do you? Do? Yeah! I was on my bike, you know—it has bald tires—and I was on my bike and at the intersection of Larch and (I think it's Larch, but anyway), I came around the bend and… .

Through such gibberish we make ourselves understood with the help of the nonverbal channel such as inflection, eye contact, and gestures. (More on delivery in Strategy 4.)

Of course, I am not advocating that we preach gibberish. Public speaking demands more order and precision than interpersonal conversation, yet public speaking should have a conversational quality. The marks of such speech are listed above: short sentences, sound effects, contractions, and so forth. It is difficult to write in that kind of style, so when you write your manuscript, speak it aloud. Hear the words you are putting on paper.

I am not implying that you should read the manuscript in the pulpit. Instead, in your study wrestle the best words onto the page, rehearse aloud a few times with the manuscript, and then step into the pulpit with only skeletal notes. Much of the language of the manuscript will come back to you, yet it will also have the flash of spontaneous thought.

### Strategy 3.5: Use Dialogue

As mentioned in Chapter 3, a surprising amount of biblical narrative is dialogue, so the genre-sensitive preacher can carry that technique directly into the sermon. The use of dialogue shows the truth and prompts the listener to collaborate, deducing what is in the heart of the character. Some fiction writers advise that dialogue should comprise a third of the novel or short story.[12] Let the characters do the talking. Not: "Paul said to the jailer that he shouldn't hurt himself." But: "Don't harm yourself!" (Acts 16:28, alt.). Look again at the passage from Alison Gerber to notice her use of brief dialogue. I count twelve short speeches.

Let's close Strategy 3 by observing how some biblical narrators use heart-revealing, pathos-stirring, plot-advancing, powerful-yet-indirect statements from characters:

- "Oh, my Lord, please send someone else." (Exod 4:13—when Moses refused to return to Egypt).
- "Behold the fire and the wood, but where is the lamb for a burnt offering?" (Gen 22:7—when Isaac helped Abraham prepare for sacrifice).
- "Do not call me Naomi; call me Mara [bitter]." (Ruth 1:20— when Naomi returned to Bethlehem).
- "O my son Absalom, my son, my son Absalom! Would I had died instead of you, O Absalom, my son, my son." (2 Sam 18:33— when David learned of Absalom's death).

The next Strategy walks arm in arm with "vivid and clear language," because in oral communication, the nonverbal element— our delivery—cannot be separated from the verbal.

## Strategy 4: Embody the Emotions

James Henning defines oral communication as "the integrated use of words, voice, and action by the speaker for the purpose of accurate and skillful communication of his [or her] ideas and feelings to a listener."[13] Strategy 4 focuses on the second and third elements in the definition, voice and action, what Edward T. Hall called the "silent language."[14]

---

12 Galli and Larson, *Preaching That Connects*, 84.

13 James H. Henning, *Improving Oral Communication* (McGraw-Hill, 1966), 7.

14 Edward T. Hall, *The Silent Language* (Doubleday, 1957; repr., Fawcett, 1968), 10.

Every introductory textbook in public speaking and homiletics devotes space to delivery, usually a chapter, but that chapter often comes last and feels perfunctory. A biblical theology of preaching tells us that we should change our attitude. That is, God has ordained that preaching be embodied. How will they hear without a preacher (Rom 10:14)? He has put the gospel into "jars of clay" (2 Cor 4:7)—the apostles, and by extension, all preachers. Amos Wilder argues in *Early Christian Rhetoric* that the incarnation is the fundamental doctrine of Christianity as Jesus took a body to represent his Father, and then preachers continued to embody the message. In turn, the authors of the New Testament chose written forms—story (gospel) and epistle—that reflect and recreate this incarnational approach to communication.[15]

Theology tells us the importance of embodied communication, and science does too. The research is conclusive: delivery matters. Thousands of studies lead to the same conclusion. For example, Donald Bligh combed the social science research to determine what helps and hinders the lecture method of instruction. Here is one of his conclusions: "There's only one thing more contagious than enthusiasm, and that's the lack of it. The way to interest a class is to display interest oneself."[16] Dynamic delivery—as measured with behaviors like gestures, eye contact, vocal variety, and speaking without a script—led to greater recall, more note taking, more positive attitudes among students, and listeners ranked those teachers more highly than blasé lecturers.

Bligh may not have been aware that rhetorician Hugh Blair also used the metaphor of infection. In 1783 he observed: "There is obviously a contagion among the passions."[17] Homiletician Robert Dabney described the same thing with this phrase: the "phenomenon of instinctive sympathy," and he called it the "orator's right arm in the work of persuasion."[18] Centuries before Blair and Dab-

---

15 Amos N. Wilder, *Early Christian Rhetoric: The Language of the Gospel* (Harvard University Press, 1971), 2.

16 Donald A. Bligh, *What's the Use of Lectures?* (Jossy-Bass, 2000), 59.

17 Hugh Blair, *Lectures on Rhetoric and Belles Lettres*, quoted in Lester Thonssen and A. Craig Baird, *Speech Criticism: The Development of Standards for Rhetorical Appraisal* (Ronald, 1948), 364.

18 Robert L. Dabney, *Sacred Rhetoric: A Course of Lectures on Preaching*

ney, Plato talked about the same rhetorical effect with the analogy of a magnet.[19] Just as the mysterious power of a magnet is transmitted through a succession of iron rings, so do the gods transmit the power of inspiration to a poet, who transmits the power to a rhapsode (oral storyteller), who then transmits the power to the audience. However we describe it—contagion, instinctive sympathy, or magnetism—experienced preachers and storytellers know that it happens. We set ourselves on fire, and the spark travels to the listeners.

The power of nonverbal communication is especially vital in conveying emotion. In fact, as much as 93% of emotional content may be conveyed through the tone of voice, eye contact, touch, and other channels of communication, especially when the two channels—verbal and nonverbal—seem to contradict each other.[20] Knapp and Hall are experts in interpersonal communication, but their maxim applies just as well to preaching: "*How* something is said is frequently *what* is said."[21] Listeners process the "how" rapidly—about a sixth of a second—so the way we embody our messages is nearly subliminal.[22] That is why Malcolm Gladwell titled his book about the accuracy of first impressions, *Blink*.[23]

In neuroscience, the phenomenon of "contagion" is called "intersubjectivity" or "mutual-mind." Mirror neurons are involved—specialized nerve cells in the brain that help us mimic one another and feel empathy. When in mutual-mind, we "synchronize human

---

(Presbyterian Committee of Publication, 1870; repr. www.onthewing.org, 2009), 247. http://www.onthewing.org/user/Dabney%20-%20Sacred%20Rhetoric.pdf.

19 Plato, *Ion*, trans. Benjamin Jowett, https://www.gutenberg.org/ebooks/1635.

20 Albert Mehrabian and Morton Wiener, "Decoding of Inconsistent Communications," *Journal of Personality and Social Psychology* 6 (1967): 109–114; Albert Mehrabian and Susan R. Ferris, "Inference of Attitudes from Nonverbal Communication in Two Channels," *Journal of Consulting Psychology* 31 (1967): 248–252.

21 Mark L. Knapp and Judith A. Hall, *Nonverbal Communication in Human Interaction*, 3rd ed. (Holt, Rinehart, & Winston, 1992), 326.

22 Jim Wilder, *Renovated: God, Dallas Willard, & the Church That Transforms* (NavPress, 2020), 36.

23 Malcolm Gladwell, *Blink: The Power of Thinking Without Thinking* (Little, Brown, and Company, 2005), 11.

thought, motivation, energy, and activities by helping two brains experience the same internal state of activation, together and in real time."[24] Most importantly for this chapter, "mutual-mind states are produced through visual cues and voice tone rather than words."[25] An example of the research behind such conclusions comes from the journal *NeuroImage*: when a person makes a facial expression or simply views someone else's facial expression, the same areas of the brain fire in both people: "Subjects spontaneously, rapidly, and covertly imitate visually presented facial expressions."[26] A similar set of experiments was done with a storyteller, concluding that "the speaker's [brain] activity is spatially and temporally coupled with the listener's activity," but the "coupling vanishes when participants fail to communicate."[27]

I could go on and on about the fascinating field of nonverbal communication, but you get the idea. Delivery matters. When preaching narratives, it is the storyteller's right arm in producing the rhetorical effects inherent in the text itself. So, how can we sharpen our delivery?[28]

"The chief requisite, then, for moving the feelings of others is … that we ourselves be moved."

Quintilian, *The Institutes of Oratory*

*Figure 8.4: Start with Yourself*

## Strategy 4.1: Start with Yourself

This strategy goes back to Strategies 1 and 2. We must pray ourselves deep into the text, exegeting with care and imagination.

24 Wilder, *Renovated*, 33.
25 Ibid, 36.
26 Andreas Hennslotter, et al. "A Common Neural Basis for Receptive and Expressive Communication of Pleasant Facial Affect," *NeuroImage* 26 (2005): 581.
27 Greg, J Stephens, et al. "Speaker-Listener Neural Coupling Underlies Successful Communication," *Proceedings of the National Academy of Sciences* 107/32 (2010): 14425–14430.
28 Specific exercises are available in Jeffrey D. Arthurs, *Devote Yourself to the Public Reading of Scripture* (Kregel, 2012), 67–104. That book also contains a video to demonstrate the principles.

Without this indispensable "strategy," the ones that follow will be fruitless; and in many ways, when we employ this "strategy," the others that follow will be superfluous.

### Strategy 4.2: Watch Yourself on Video

This is painful, but there is no better schoolmaster for delivery because speakers do not perceive themselves the way listeners perceive them. When we watch ourselves on a screen, however, we get the listener's perspective. For instance, speakers often feel that they project with plenty of volume and crisp articulation, but the video tells another tale. The use of a pause may feel like a Grand Canyon of silence, but the video reveals that the canyon was not grand at all. The same is true for our gestures, eye contact, and facial expressions. We tend to feel we are more animated than we actually are.

| Which of the following words describes your pastor's preaching? | | |
|---|---|---|
| | Pastors' Response | Congregations' Response |
| Energetic | 43% | 29% |
| Conversational | 46% | 22% |

*Figure 8.5: Matching Our Perceptions and Listeners' Perceptions*

### Strategy 4.3: Speak Extemporaneously

Stated negatively, do not read your sermon from a manuscript. Few people can leverage the nonverbal channel when reading from the printed page. Their eyes are down, not up. Their movement is inhibited, not free. Their spontaneity is constrained, not natural. Their voices are cadenced, progressing at the rate that their eyes take in the words, not moving at the rate of thought. In Wayne McDill's memorable phrase: "Paper is a very poor conductor of electricity."[29]

---

29 Wayne V. McDill, *The Moment of Truth: A Guide to Effective Sermon Delivery* (B&H, 1999), 145.

Preaching without the comfort of a manuscript can make us feel that we are walking the high wire, but it can be done. Imagine how would you feel if we made extemporaneous speaking the law of the land? Well, they did! In 1667 in Bern, Switzerland, church authorities instituted the "Bern Preacher Act" which required that preachers "must not read [their sermons] in front of the congregation from notes on paper, which is a mockery to have to watch and which takes away all fruit and grace from the preacher in the eyes of the listeners."[30]

To be clear: I *do* recommend that we write out a manuscript because of the advantages described above, and that we practice aloud with the manuscript, but then reduce the script to skeletal notes. Those will be enough to keep you on track and help you recall some of the fine wording from the manuscript. This is the best of both worlds—vivid and precise language along with spontaneity and audience-connection.

But the question remains: how can I traverse the high wire with just one page of notes as a skimpy safety net? That question was asked in antiquity as well as in the modern age. One of the "canons" (major divisions) of classical rhetoric was "memory." They did not memorize their orations in the sense of word-for-word recitation. Rather they internalized the carefully prepared content and then recalled it with the help of visual images. They developed a technique called the "memory palace." The orator would associate ideas with locations in a palace, and as he walked around the palace in his imagination, he would recall the points of his speech in their proper order. Dave McClellan incorporates those insights into homiletics with "roadmapping."[31] The technique works with the brain's preference for remembering pictures rather than abstractions. Simple visual symbols represent the points to be made—symbols such as such as the diagram of plot, arrows, traffic signs, mathematical signs, and emojis like a heart or frowning face. Figure 8.6 develops this technique with suggestions on how to preach extemporaneously.

---

30  In Hans Van der Geest, *Presence in the Pulpit: The Impact of Personality in Preaching*, trans. John Douglas W. Stott (John Knox, 1981), 47.

31  Dave McClellan, *Preaching by Ear: Speaking God's Truth from the Inside Out* (Weaver, 2014), 131–137.

- Organize your material with a natural, easy-to-follow flow. (Narrative-preaching is ideal for this.)
- Use visual symbols.
- Write a manuscript and include the symbols in the margin.
- Practice with the manuscript, eventually only glancing at it.
- Reduce the manuscript to brief notes. Include the symbols.
- Take a walk and speak the sermon with only your notes. After the walk, see if you forgot anything.
- Preach with only notes. If you forget something, don't fret. You are the only one who knows.

*Figure 8.6: How to Preach Extemporaneously*

## Strategy 4.4: Observe Good Speakers

We can learn a lot from each other, and sermons captured on video are as easy to find today as leaves on my front lawn in autumn. You might like to observe speakers from a different gender, culture, ethnicity, era, or denomination. Take stock of things that you see like pausing, facial expression, and posture. Pick out two things that you could do yourself. Be careful not to imitate the speaker; rather, incorporate a couple of their strengths into your own style. You might also like to listen to Scripture readers or watch public speakers or even comedians. What can you learn from expert speakers? Figure 8.7 gives some more ideas for improving delivery, and 8.8 offers a checklist for self-assessment in delivery.

The next chapter is devoted to a single strategy, the third-person narrative sermon. This is the heart of genre-sensitive preaching from narrative.

- Mime a biblical story—no words, just actions. Convey the events (the plot) and the emotions.

- Speak one sentence and see how many meanings you can convey by your voice: "Oh, I didn't know you would be here."

- Speak one narrative passage, Luke 10:38 –42, conveying different nuances when Jesus rebukes Martha for her grumpy service. In separate readings, show Jesus's irritation, compassion, humor, and amazement.

- Set the pulpit aside. Practice your sermon with nothing between you and the congregation. Deliver it this way too.

- Use five distinct gestures to convey various affective meanings on this sentence: "Woman, I do not know him" (Luke 22:57): Accusing – Pleading – Reasoning – Defending – Scoffing.

*Figure 8.7: Exercises for Delivery Practice*

| Technique | Effective | Needs Work |
|---|---|---|
| Step up confidently and begin with authority. | | |
| Establish eye contact before you start speaking. | | |
| Sound natural, not memorized. | | |
| Use limited, practical notes. | | |
| Refer to notes only occasionally. | | |
| Pause. Do not be afraid of silence. | | |
| Stand tall. Do not lean, cross legs, sway, etc. | | |
| Avoid verbal fillers (uhm, so, you know …). | | |
| Project to the last row. | | |
| Vary your gestures to match the verbal content. | | |

| | | |
|---|---|---|
| Use vocal variety and color to express emotion. | | |
| Wake up your face. Convey emotion. | | |
| End conclusively. Do not trail off or drag on. | | |

*Figure 8.8: Delivery Checklist*

## For Further Study

- Arthurs, Jeffrey D. *Devote Yourself to the Public Reading of Scripture: The Transforming Power of the Well-Spoken Word.* Kregel, 2012.
- Arthurs, Jeffrey. "No Notes, Lot of Notes, Brief Notes: The Pros and Cons of Extemporaneous and Manuscript Delivery." Pages 600–606, in *The Art and Craft of Biblical Preaching.* Edited by Haddon Robinson and Craig Brian Larson. Zondervan: 2005.
- Galli, Mark, and Craig Brian Larson. *Preaching that Connects: Using Journalistic Techniques to Add Impact.* Zondervan, 1994.
- Mathewson, Steven D. *The Art of Preaching Old Testament Narrative.* 2nd ed. Baker, 2021.
- McClellan, Dave. *Preaching By Ear: Speaking God's Truth from the Inside Out.* Weaver Books, 2014.
- McDill, Wayne V. *The Moment of Truth: A Guide to Effective Sermon Delivery.* B&H, 1999.

### Talk about It

Discuss this passage from Peter Marshall's "Were You There?"[32] Comment on his effective style and suggest things you might do differently.

> The morning sun had been up for some hours over the city of David. Already pilgrims and visitors pouring in through the gates.... There were the aged, stooped with years, muttering to themselves as they pushed through the throngs, and there were

---

32  Galli and Larson, *Preaching That Connects*, 97.

children playing in the streets, calling to each other in shrill voices. There were men and women too, carrying burdens, baskets of vegetables, casks of wine, water bags. And there were tradesmen with their tools.

## Dig Deeper

Watch the video that accompanies Arthurs, *Devote Yourself to the Public Reading of Scripture.*

## Practice

- Write a cinquain on this topic: preaching.
- Re-write this cluttered and flaccid sentence with no more than twelve words (from Galli and Larson, *Preaching That Connects*, 93–94). It is 26 words, uses passive voice, and is boring.

  My life has been affected by the relentless creativity of God in such a consistent manner that I'd like to share with you what I'm learning.

- Reduce your next sermon manuscript to one page of notes. Go for it!

# 9

# Strategies for Form, Part One

*There ought to be such a method of
preaching upon the narrative portions of
Scripture as should be distinctively appropriate to narrative.*[1]

John Broadus

*If you want to motivate, persuade, or be
remembered, start with a story of human
struggle and eventual triumph. It will
capture people's hearts—first by attracting
their brains.*[2]

Paul J. Zak

AVING LAID OUT some general strategies for saying what
the text says and doing what the text does, we turn now
to the issue of form—the shape of the sermon. Will the
sermon be composed primarily of propositional points, or will it
be composed primarily of story? As I have stated, I feel that when
we preach from narrative, our first option for form should be the
third-person narrative sermon. My reasoning is simple: God has
inscripturated his Word as story, so expository preachers re-com-
municate that Word as story.

---

[1] John A. Broadus, *A Treatise on the Preparation and Delivery of Sermons*,
20th ed. (Barbee & Smith, 1894), 304.

[2] Paul J. Zak, "Why Your Brain Loves Good Storytelling," *Harvard Business
Review* (Oct. 28, 2014): https://hbr.org/2014/why-your-brain-loves-good-story-
telling. Accessed January 10, 2020.

In addition to this theological rationale—the nature of revelation—story also offers psychological benefits for those who would teach and persuade. When we imagine characters doing things in a certain locale (three elements of the genre—character, plot, and setting), we use the same regions of the brain as when we actually witness or do those things. Heath and Heath compare listening to a story to practicing inside a flight simulator.[3] To learn to operate a space shuttle, such practice is not as good as actually flying the shuttle, but it is the next best thing. In the same way, when we hear stories of how people overcome problems, we practice life. According to the flight simulator theory, when a congregation hears about Zacchaeus up in the tree desperately seeking to see Jesus (assuming that the story is told with concrete language and effective delivery), they use the same brain processes as if they were present at the scene. Similarly, as we saw in Chapter 8 with Campbell's theory of "vivacity," story uses an "operation of the mind" similar to actual experience.

So, tell the story! Strategy 5 gives advice on how to structure the sermon as story.

## Strategy 5: Use a Third-Person Narrative

In a third-person story the narrator speaks about "he," "she," "it," or "they," rather than "I" and "we." The preacher might begin as Haddon Robinson does with his sermon about David and Bathsheba:

> His name was David. He was a king reigning in the city of Jerusalem. When you say that David was a king, you mean that he was a twenty-four carat king. He wasn't a desert chieftain followed by a band of bandits… . No, David was a king… . As far as the eye could see, as far as the foot could walk, David was the man in control.[4]

---

3 Chip Heath and Dan Heath, *Made to Stick: Why Some Ideas Survive and Others Die* (Random House, 2007), 212–214.
4 Haddon W. Robinson, "Mid-Life Crisis: Problem Ancient and Modern." Unpub. sermon, preached at the Portland Pastor's Conference, Portland, OR, 1996.

Similarly, Rev. E. V. Hill speaks in the third person as he provides background to the story of Moses at the burning bush:

> Imagine the ghetto section of Egypt. A great people had been enslaved here for hundreds of years. Imagine how they had prayed and prayed, daily making known their supplications, their hurt, and their sorrows. Amidst an idolatrous people they had continued to pray to the one, true God.[5]

Both examples use an omniscient narrator, and that is most common with the third-person sermon, but you could also use a limited point of view wherein the narrator knows the thoughts of just one character. The narrator could even be restricted to surface appearances, simply recounting what would be readily seen by a spectator.

Both examples also use past tense, but sometimes third-person storytelling is done in present tense. Thus, Robinson might have said, "His name *is* David. He *is* a king in Jerusalem." Present tense can add a sense of immediacy to the story. Matthew Kim does this with his sermon on Jonah: "As Jonah sloshes around inside of the fish, he recites prayers from the book of Psalms... . Having spent days in the fish's belly, Jonah finally comes to his senses and obeys God."[6]

We can break down this grand approach—the third-person narrative sermon—into some sub-strategies that help us do what the text does.

### Strategy 5.1: Follow the Plot

We have seen the rhetorical charm of plot, and the most natural way to reproduce it is simply by following the plot. Good storytellers unambiguously state the conflict and then drive it through

---

5 E. V. Hill, "God's Answer," unpub. sermon, preached at Western Seminary, Portland, OR, 1985.

6 Matthew M. Kim, "Jonah's Shady Outlook from His Sunny Lookout," in *Models for Biblical Preaching: Expository Sermon from the Old Testament*, ed. Haddon W. Robinson and Patricia Batten (Baker: 2014), 160.

the climax. For example, the story of Hagar might announce the conflict bluntly: "Her mistress hated her. Yes, hated. I know that's a strong word, but it is the right word. Sarai hated Hagar, and she looked for a chance to get even." In your exegesis, identify the conflict and then lay out the plot through its "stair steps" for each complication. With the example of Hagar, each stair step will deal with the conflict between Sarai and her until it is resolved either as a "comedy" or "tragedy." Keep the background short so that you can get to the conflict as soon as possible. That's where the magic dwells.

The story of Zacchaeus does not present riveting conflict of physical action like David and Goliath, or even Sarai and Hagar, but psychological conflict is present when Luke says that the *architelōnēs* wanted to see Jesus. As I have argued, this "seeing" was more than curiosity. It is a shorthand way of saying that Zacchaeus was wrestling with rejection from his own people and guilt from his own conscience. He was looking for acceptance and forgiveness, even if those motives were slumbering. Nevertheless, his desire to see Jesus was hindered on every side: he was a sinner, he was short, he probably balked at the indignity of running and climbing a tree, and the crowd was against him. Those complications deal with a single conflict—the desire to see Jesus—which the climax resolves. He did indeed meet Jesus, in a way that exceeded his expectations and produced profound repentance.

Keep the plot moving forward steadily. Remember that the audience asks, "What happens next?" By driving the plot, we can leverage the story's formal excellence. At times, it is permissible to make short digressions from the plot to explain some exegetical data, but keep the digressions short. Notice how Steve Mathewson does this in his sermon on Ehud (Judg 3:12–30):

> The sword crafted by Ehud is short. This is not the normal word for an eighteen-inch sword. Old Testament scholar Lawson Younger argues that the sword's length is only a foot long. The sword is also double-edged, literally "double mouthed." It's not the kind you use in battle to hack someone. It is designed more for a jab and slice.[7]

---

7 Steve Mathewson, "The Story of the Left-Handed Assassin and the Obese

Briefly placing the plot on hold can also be done when the preacher wants to apply the truth. Patricia Batten does this in a narrative sermon from Psalm 73. In mid-sermon she pushes pause to speak pastorally to her congregation:

> Maybe you've had your own Psalm 73 moments when you've doubted God's goodness. We'd never admit it here, in this place … [as] we've sat in these pews week after week praising God and thanking God, and has there ever been a Sunday when you've said to yourself, "I don't know if I believe this anymore. God's goodness? Not in my life!"[8]

It is possible to put the plot on hold for even longer by using the technique Eugene Lowry calls "alternating the story": the preacher tells part of the biblical narrative, leaving the audience with a cliff hanger; then the preacher begins a modern story, perhaps a testimony; then returns to the story and the next cliff; then back to the modern story; and so forth.[9]

If you have punctuated the plot of the biblical story with exegetical data, illustrations, applications, or even a modern story, or even if you have *not* punctuated the plot but have told a "pure" story, when you have climbed the stair steps and arrived at the climax, make it climactic. Just as we state the conflict unambiguously ("Her mistress hated her"), so we should state the climax plainly to show how it all turns out and who "wins." The rhetoric of plot depends on gripping conflict driven to a tension-releasing climax.

Robinson's narrative sermon on David, Bathsheba, and Uriah focuses on the conflict between David and God. David abuses his power, sins against Bathsheba and Uriah, and tries to cover his sin, but his sin is first and foremost against God. He has alienated himself from God, and as Robinson says, lived for a year or so "in

---

King," in *Models for Biblical Preaching*, 44.

8 Patricia Batten, "The Story of the Worship Leader Who Lost His Song," in *Models for Biblical Preaching*, 65.

9 Eugene L. Lowry, *How to Preach a Parable: Designs for Narrative Sermons* (Abingdon, 1989), 142–170. Austin B. Tucker also discusses this form in *The Preacher as Storyteller: The Power of Narrative in the Pulpit* (B&H, 2008), 86–87.

the far country." But then the Lord sends Nathan to confront him. Here is the climax in Robinson's third-person re-telling:

> The color drained from David's face. His hands grew cold. He felt his head swim, his throat grow dry. Nathan had stopped speaking. His eyes were on the floor. Nathan the prophet was silent—he had spoken the truth. Nathan the friend was silent— he had said enough. With a voice choked and strained David finally spoke. Gone was the confidence of the brave soldier, gone was the authority of the powerful king.... David replied only, "I have sinned against the Lord."[10]

The first sub-strategy—follow the plot—is the primary mark of a third-person narrative sermon. But remember that the umbrella tree is broad and has plenty of room for elements from traditional sermons. My advice about punctuating the flow of the plot with short digressions has already shown one example of this. The next sub-strategy offers another way to incorporate elements of the traditional sermon.

### Strategy 5.2: If Helpful, Use a Traditional Introduction or Conclusion

Sometimes the sermon will begin *in media res* ("Jesus stepped out of the boat onto the shore of the Lake. A man ran up to him, wild and crazed, shouting and gesturing... ."), but at other times it might start with a traditional introduction. By "traditional" I mean the kind of introduction that typically starts a sermon—one that gains attention, surfaces need, and leads to the big idea or first point of the sermon. Traditional introductions often use a current event, story, quotation, or rhetorical question ("Good morning, friends. Last week I finished a wonderful biography of Dr. Martin Luther King, Jr. I learned that when he faced one of the most dangerous seasons in his long struggle for civil rights, he wrote the following words... .") One advantage of using a traditional introduction

---

10 Haddon W. Robinson, "Mid-Life Crisis: Problem Ancient and Modern." Unpub. sermon, preached at the Portland Pastor's Conference, Portland, OR, 1996.

before re-telling the biblical story, is that it makes an immediate connection to the listeners. Neuroscientist Richard Cox says that such connection is vital: "The brain, without any conscious intent, determines very early in a sermon whether the mind's lights will come on or will short out and turn off."[11]

Another advantage is accrued if the congregation is not familiar with narrative sermons. They may resist a sermon that is "merely" a story, so a standard introduction can help defuse a bewildered or negative reaction. Sunukjian uses a traditional introduction before retelling the story of Esther:

> There's a book in the Bible where the name of God is never mentioned—the Book of Esther. But even though God's name is mentioned nowhere in the book, you sense his presence everywhere, controlling what happens. It's like a dollhouse where the top has been removed and some big father can lean in, move the people around, rearrange the furniture, and do anything he wants. That huge father does not walk around in the dollhouse, yet he controls everything that happens.… . I would like to tell you the story of Esther through the eyes of one of the minor characters of the book. The man is on the palace staff, an attendant to the king. He's on the inside. He knows everything that's going on. How would this man, who never hears the name of God and yet sees everything that happens, view it? [pause] My name is Harbona.[12]

E. K. Bailey also uses a traditional introduction in his sermon on Zacchaeus:

> One of the benefits that we experience growing up in a local church is the various assortment of songs, rhymes, games, and

---

11 Richard H. Cox, *Rewiring Your Preaching: How the Brain Processes Sermons* (IVP, 2012), 23.

12 Donald Sunukjian, "A Night in Persia," in *Biblical Sermons: How Twelve Preachers Apply the Principles of Biblical Preaching*, ed. Haddon W. Robinson (Baker, 1989), 71–80. https://www.preachingtoday.com/sermons/sermons/2005/august/0364.html. Notice that Sunukjian's sermon is first-person, not third. We will cover the first-person form in the next chapter.

couplets which indelibly stamp the names of biblical characters upon the fabric of our memories. [Bailey then recalls the Sunday school song about Zacchaeus, the "wee little man."] I've always wondered what drove Zacchaeus to climb that tree.... In order to answer this and many other questions, I invite you to take a journey with me.[13]

The use of a traditional *conclusion* is also an option for the narrative preacher. After the story is completed, the preacher might speak directly and pastorally to the congregation to reflect on what they have heard. When the sermon ends with direct discourse rather than narrative, it may feel more like a "real" sermon. Bailey ends with a traditional conclusion. Ninety percent of the sermon is retelling the story of Zacchaeus, but then in the final moment, he says:

Jesus always makes a difference when he goes home with you. In fact, if he doesn't go home with you, he doesn't go anywhere with you—because Jesus knows that who you are at home is who and what you really are. As Zacchaeus and Jesus walked away with their arms around each other, I could hear Zacchaeus singing:
*"Jesus saves to the utmost.*
*He will pick you up and turn you around.*
*Hallelujah ... yes, Jesus saves."*[14]

With a traditional conclusion, the preacher can even develop a few points in outline form, thus combining narrative preaching with propositional. The preacher might offer three "lessons," or two "take-aways" from the story. I did this when I preached a third-person sermon on Exodus 2, Moses in the bulrushes. For a few minutes at the end of the sermon, I offered three "reflections" with the last one being Christo-centric: (1) God hears, remembers, sees, and knows. (2) God uses us in his plan to deliver others. (3) God sent his Son to be the ultimate deliverer.[15]

---

13  E. K. Bailey and Warren W. Wiersbe, *Preaching in Black and White: What We Can Learn from Each Other* (Zondervan, 2002), 142.

14  Bailey and Warren, *Preaching in Black and White*, 149–150.

15  Jeffrey D. Arthurs, "A Basket—God's Deliverance," unpub. sermon,

The next strategy is related to the previous one and again shows the flexibility of the third-person narrative sermon.

### Strategy 5.3: Frame the Big Idea and Determine Where to Place It

Even when most of the sermon is story, it should still communicate the author's primary theological and ethical intention. Articulating those intentions in a single sentence keeps the sermon on track for you and your hearers. A narrative sermon without a central idea is a Rorschach's blot inviting listeners to make of it what they will.[16] Robinson calls the central idea (or thesis) the "big idea."[17] Donald Sunukjian calls it the "take home truth,"[18] and I have heard it referred to as "the sermon in a sentence."

On the other hand, as I have emphasized in this book, the artistic nature of narrative resists distillation. Therefore, how can the expository preacher who is committed to authorial intention—content and form—communicate a central idea and apply it to the listeners? Here are some options.

---

preached at Crossbridge, Lexington, MA, January 2020.

16 Fred Craddock, a homiletical genius, started the tsunami of approbation for inductive and narrative preaching with his classics *As One Without Authority* and *Overhearing the Gospel*, but Craddock offered indirection as a response to Christendom in United States. Everyone, so it was assumed, had at least passing acquaintance with the gospel and church attendance was just the same-old, same-old. For the gospel to surprise such an audience, so that they could hear it fresh in its beauty and power, Craddock offered induction and indirection—overhearing the gospel—rather than a homiletic that shoveled the truth in blunt pronouncements. However, we no longer live in Christendom. Biblical illiteracy is rampant and the cord that tethers us to Christian doctrine is frayed and ready to snap. Even Craddock said that "forms of preaching should be as varied as the forms of rhetoric in the New Testament" (*As One Without Authority* [Abingdon, 1971], 53), and "The wise course to follow is keep both direct and indirect [forms] ... present in the content and style of our communicating" (*Overhearing the Gospel*, rev. and exp. ed. [Chalice, 2002], 74). Thus, this book seeks ways to leverage the power of story while still teaching doctrine with its ethical implications.

17 Haddon W. Robinson, *Biblical Preaching: The Development and Delivery of Expository Messages*, 3rd ed. (Baker, 2014), 15–26.

18 Donald R. Sunukjian, *Invitation to Biblical Preaching: Proclaiming Truth with Clarity and Relevance* (Kregel, 2007), 65–83.

## Deductive

This means that the preacher states the idea early in the sermon, often in a traditional introduction: "Today we will look at the story of X. It teaches us Z." Such an approach gains clarity but loses suspense and collaboration. An approach that is less blunt, but still deductive, is to articulate the subject of the big idea (the question that drives the sermon), but not the complement (the answer to the question). Thus, in my sermon on Acts 9, the conversion of Saul, I broach the subject of the story without giving away the whole idea. The subject is "How did God encounter and convert Saul?

> When we think of Paul, we tend to think of him as "the apostle Paul," author of the New Testament, missionary, and theologian; deeply devoted to God and tender-hearted toward people. But he was "Paul" for only half of his life. Before he was "Paul," he was "Saul": brilliant Pharisee, ruthless persecutor, and enemy of Jesus. How did he go from "Saul" to "Paul"? As Calvin said, the wolf became a sheep and then a shepherd. How did that happen?[19]

## Inductive

An inductive sermon saves the big idea until the end. The details of the story show the idea and gradually lead to it before stating it plainly. For example, the big idea of my Acts 9 sermon is, "When God encounters us and we are converted, the grace of God turns us around." As you saw in the paragraph above, I imply that idea in the introduction, and then most of the sermon shows that truth with details about Saul's hatred, encounter with the risen Christ, repentance, and conversion. Then in the climax, I state plainly:

> Ananias laid his hands on Saul, and immediately something like scales fell from his eyes, and he could see. Saul got up, ate, and

---

19 Jeffrey D. Arthurs, "The Wolf Became a Shepherd," unpub. sermon, preached at Northridge Community Church, Portland, OR, March 1998.

regained his strength. He was a new man, inside and out. The grace of God turned him around, one hundred and eighty degrees. This was the start of new life. Has the grace of God turned you around? You have not overshot his capacity to forgive. Behold, he stands at the door knocking; if anyone hears his voice and opens the door, he will come in and turn you around.

## Scattered

At various moments during the narrative, you might weave the big idea into the flow of the plot. For example, in the middle of the Acts 9 sermon I might insert:

> Look at the compassion and power of God! We worship a mighty God, don't we? He took this self-righteous, hateful man and turned him around. One hundred and eighty degrees! That's what the grace of God does, you know. It stops us in our tracks and puts us on another track.

Sometimes we can put the central idea into the mouth of a character:

> Ananias took Saul by the shoulders, looked him in the eye, and said, "God has rescued you, brother Saul. He has stopped you in your tracks and redeemed your soul. The grace of God has turned you around. Now serve him with a glad heart in newness of life.

## Implied

With this option, the preacher does not state the idea. Instead, he or she prompts the listeners to infer it. This takes homiletical skill, but the benefits are great. Director Stanley Kubrick reflects on his own medium of film: "When you say something directly, it is simply not as potent as it is when you allow people to discover it for themselves."[20] When listeners collaborate with the preacher

---

20 Stanley Kubrick, "Kubrick's Greatest Gamble," *Time* (December 15, 1975): 72.

to mentally articulate the main idea, attention rises, retention increases, and change of behavior deepens. Sunukjian's sermon on Esther does this masterfully. If stated bluntly, the big idea would be: "God controls the affairs of kingdoms and the lives of individuals"; but Sunukjian does not take that kind of blunt approach. Instead, he prompts the listeners to collaborate with him. At the end of the sermon the narrator, a pagan, states: "Those Jews—they sure are lucky!" The audience responds silently: "Luck? That wasn't luck! That was the sovereign hand of God guiding the affairs of the kingdom and the lives of the individuals."

Having arranged the sermon according to the plot of the story, perhaps adding a traditional introduction or conclusion, and having framed the big idea and decided where to place it, you are well on your way to preaching a genre-sensitive sermon from narrative. Surround this form with an ensemble of prayerful and imaginative exegesis, concrete language, and fervent delivery, and let the sermon sing.

The next chapter discusses some more forms that can be found under the broad umbrella tree called "narrative preaching." The third-person sermon may be our standard form for genre-sensitive preaching, but other forms also can recreate the rhetorical dynamics of biblical narrative.

## For Further Study

- Craddock, Fred B. *Overhearing the Gospel.* Rev. and exp. ed. Chalice, 2002.
- Mathewson, Steven D. *The Art of Preaching Old Testament Narrative.* 2nd ed. Baker, 2021.
- Larsen, David L. *Telling the Old, Old Story: The Art of Narrative Preaching.* Kregel, 1995.

### Talk about It

Has your congregation heard a narrative sermon? If not, how do you think they would respond to one? If you anticipate a negative reaction ("That was cute but not a *real* sermon!"), do you think that ending with a traditional conclusion would help them feel that they had heard a real sermon?

## Dig Deeper

This book argues that preachers should take the form of the text into account, as well as the content; so, would it ever be appropriate to preach a narrative sermon from a non-narrative text? If you answer yes, when would it be appropriate to do so?

## Practice

Write three short paragraphs summarizing how you would preach the story of Elijah on Mount Carmel:

- "Straight narrative" (no traditional introduction or conclusion, implying rather than stating the big idea, few if any digressions from the plot for illustrations and application).
- "Modified narrative" (using a traditional introduction or conclusion).
- "Mixed narrative" (concluding the sermon with a few minutes of traditional, propositional points).

# 10

## Strategies for Form, Part Two

*No single sermon form has God's stamp
of approval on it saying, "Accept no
substitutes."*[1]
Haddon Robinson and Torrey Robinson

*Most methods, however exciting and
promising, are most effective when
used selectively and among a variety of
styles.... No one wins all races with the
same horse.*[2]
Fred Craddock

*So we'll live, and pray, and sing, and tell
old tales.... As if we were God's spies.*
Shakespeare, King Lear, 5.3.11–17

### Strategy 6: Expand Your Creativity

NO INTERNATIONAL SYMPOSIUM of experts has specified
what qualifies as a "narrative sermon." I have argued that
the third-person narrative should be our standard form
because of its flexibility and adherence to the shape of the text, but

---

1 Haddon W. Robinson and Torrey W. Robinson, *It's All in How You Tell It:
Preaching First-Person Expository Messages* (Baker, 2003), 11.

2 Fred B. Craddock, *Overhearing the Gospel*, rev. and exp. ed. (Chalice,
2002), 88.

in this chapter we look at other options to do what the text does, other ways to preach with qualities like suspense and resolution, concrete language, emotion, and artistry.[3]

### Strategy 6.1: Create a First-Person Narrative

A popular choice for preaching narrative is the first-person narrative sermon, also called a "dramatic monologue." Like the third-person sermon, this form features plot, character, and setting more than propositions, but its distinguishing characteristic resides in point of view. It tells the story from the perspective of one of the characters. Nearly all the advice in Chapters 7–9 applies to this form also, such as the use of concrete language and following the plot, but the first-person narrative is unique in some ways, so this sub-strategy gives special attention to the features of this kind of story.[4]

Before getting into "how to," I will first acknowledge and address some concerns you may have. After all, taking on the persona of a character for the purpose of expository preaching blends the arts of acting and homiletics. Some congregations may be confused or annoyed by a form so different from what they are used to. If that is true of your church, then skip to the next section. No sermon form is worth derailing the ministry of the Word, yet perhaps you should not assume the congregation's antipathy too quickly. The dramatic monologue can be a delightful and disarming ingredient in your homiletical stew. You might experiment with the first-person form by first presenting a monologue to the youth group; if that goes well, then try a non-worship setting such as a father-daughter

---

3  J. Kent Edwards, *Effective First-Person Biblical Preaching: The Steps from Text to Narrative Sermon* (Zondervan, 2005), 126.

4  Much has been written about this popular form. Three books stand out because they emphasize exposition along with creativity: Edwards, *Effective First-Person*; Robinson and Robinson, *It's All in How You Tell It*; and Stephen Chapin Garner, *Getting into Character: The Art of First-Person Narrative Preaching* (Brazos, 2008). Two articles also value exposition: Todd H. Hilkemann, "Preaching Expository Character Narrative Sermons," https://www.preaching-today.com/skills/2021/preaching-expository-character-narrative-sermons.html; Jeffrey D. Arthurs, "Performing the Story: How to Preach First Person Narrative Sermons," *Preaching* (March/April 1997): 30–35.

banquet; and then try it on Christmas or Easter when people's appreciation of the arts is high; and the first time you try it on Sunday morning, use a standard introduction and conclusion, as we discussed in the previous chapter. This makes the message feel more like a "sermon."

Another concern is that this form tempts the preacher to feature psychology more than theology. Imagination can flirt with fantasy. As we have seen, the Bible's stories are laconic, and their primary purpose is to communicate theology, so good exegesis must ground the first-person sermon. Edwards is convinced that this form is a legitimate and powerful choice for the expository preacher, yet even he warns, "Creative presentation of the text is no excuse for sloppy interpretation of the text."[5]

A third concern deals with application. Drama does not lend itself to pastoral exhortation, so with the first-person format application is likely to be subtle and inductive, prompting the listeners to collaborate with the preacher to contemplate how the story relates to them. However, direct application is possible even with the first-person sermon:

- **The character himself/herself can apply the truth.** Having the first-person narrator make application can seem contrived, but Haddon Robinson pulls it off with pathos and skill in "The Broken Heart of David Jessison," the story of Absalom's rebellion against his father.[6] Robinson tells the story from David's perspective. In the second half of the sermon David reflects on his poor parenting, suggesting that the listeners can "feast on his carcass." The narrator offers two points, although he does not overtly label them: children need the presence of a father, and children need the godly example of a father.
- An easier choice is to **end with a traditional conclusion.** Here the narrator ends the story and signals a change by pausing, moving to a different location, breaking and re-establishing eye

---

5 J. Kent Edwards, unpub. lecture notes, quoted in Robinson and Robinson, *It's All in How You Tell It*, 41.

6 Haddon W. Robinson, "The Broken Heart of David Jessison," unpub. sermon, preached at the Portland Pastor's Conference, Portland, OR, 1994. See Appendix 2.

contact, or setting aside a prop or garment. Then the preacher-as-self can offer reflections on the story. Alice Mathews does this with the story of Mary of Bethany.[7] Mathews concludes the monologue and then speaking as herself, reflects: "When people really see a life poured out for Christ, they never fully appreciate it. It looks like fanaticism or waste. But … when we truly know [Jesus] as the resurrection and the life, we are moved to give him all that we are, all that we have."

- A variation on the traditional conclusion is to have **someone else make the application.** The preacher-as-storyteller might exit the stage, and a partner could then wrap it up, even sharing some propositional points.

Having acknowledged some concerns, I would like to put in a good work for this form. When done well, it can be a delightful way to open a text, hold attention, and give yourself and your listeners a break from the ecclesial routine. When might we choose this form?

### When the text is first-person

This is rare in Scripture, but Nehemiah, Daniel 4, and the "we" sections of Acts use first-person. Other texts are not "pure" narrative, but they also possess elements of autobiography. As we seek to do what the text does, we have warrant to follow suit.

---

- Revelation, when John encounters Jesus and observes events in heaven.
- Joshua 14, as the leader of Israel reflects on his long life.
- Job.
- Sections of epistles such as Galatians 1–2, Philippians 2–3, and most of 2 Corinthians.
- Psalms linked to specific circumstances, as summarized in the superscriptions, such as 51, 54, 59, and 63.
- Prophets, such as Jeremiah.

---

*Figure 10.1 Non-narrative texts with Autobiographical Elements*

---

7 Alice Mathews, "Mary of Bethany," in Edwards, *Effective First-Person*, 162–164.

### When the audience needs a new perspective

The text may be overly familiar or the occasion, such as Christmas or Easter, may feel overly predictable. In those cases, Craddock's counsel is warranted—the audience needs to "overhear" the Word.[8] Buttry is a master of finding a new angle with monologues such as the testimony of Thomas on Jesus's resurrection; a letter from Mary to Elizabeth on the incarnation; and the testimony of Pontius Pilate on the substitutionary atonement.[9] With the story of Pilate, Buttry catches the audience with this brief, traditional introduction: "I'm not in the habit of letting an unbeliever preach from the pulpit, but I'm going to make an exception today.... May I introduce you to Pontius Pilate?"[10]

Besides giving a text a fresh coat of paint, the first-person sermon can get around defenses. I discovered that the first time I heard this form. The sermon was on Ruth 2 from the perspective of Boaz. The preacher challenged the listeners to remain pure in their relationships with the opposite sex. Afterwards I asked the preacher why he chose that form (he had a reputation as a steady Bible teacher). He responded: "Well, I had some things to say to the single people of the church, and I thought that they would receive the exhortation better if it came from Boaz instead of me."

Pastors often ask the following questions about practical implementation of the first-person narrative:

### Do I need to "act"?

Not necessarily, but the answer depends on what you mean by "act." A first-person narrator needs to feel and embody the emotions of the story, but not necessarily take on the character's mannerisms. Also, if by "acting" you have in mind costume, make up, and set, the answer again is: not necessarily.

---

8  Craddock, *Overhearing the Gospel*, 15–30.

9  Daniel L. Buttry, *First-Person Preaching: Bringing New Life to Biblical Stories* (Judson, 1998), 31–37, 47–53, 39–45.

10  Buttry, *First-Person Preaching*, 39.

If you have the time, skill, and opportunity, you may want to lean toward the "acting" end of the continuum; for a Sunday service most of us will lean toward the other end. An example is Don Sunukjian's "A Night in Persia."[11] A court official named Harbona is the narrator, and as I mentioned in the previous chapter, the power of this sermon is in point of view more than characterization. That is, Harbona is an unbeliever, and it is delightful to witness God's sovereignty through the perspective of one who feels that the Jews were simply "lucky." Sunukjian is excellent at delivering the emotions of the story, but he wears no costume, does not speak with an accent, and does not adopt mannerisms. But he does push toward the right side of the continuum with another dramatic monologue as Mephibosheth, the crippled son of Jonathan.[12] The narrator enters with crutches, sits down, sets aside the crutches, and then relates the whole story while seated. When the story is over, he picks up the crutches and limps off. All the way on the right side of the continuum is Dean Jones's "Saint John in Exile," a one-man show of the aged apostle on Patmos with full staging, make up, and costume.[13]

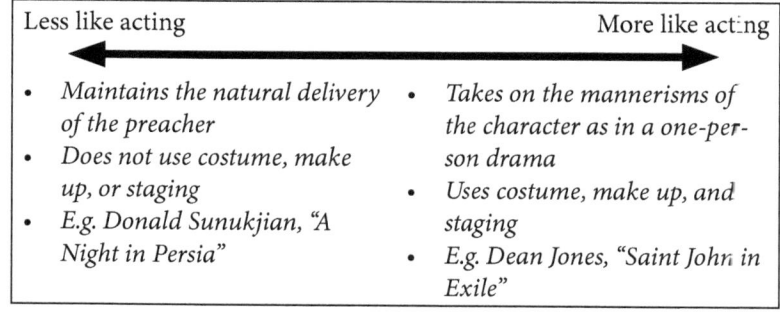

| Less like acting | More like acting |
| --- | --- |
| • Maintains the natural delivery of the preacher<br>• Does not use costume, make up, or staging<br>• E.g. Donald Sunukjian, "A Night in Persia" | • Takes on the mannerisms of the character as in a one-person drama<br>• Uses costume, make up, and staging<br>• E.g. Dean Jones, "Saint John in Exile" |

Figure 10.2: First-Person Narrative as "Acting"

---

11 Donald R. Sunukjian, "A Night in Persia," in *Biblical Sermons: How Twelve Preachers Apply the Principles of Biblical Preaching*, ed. Haddon W. Robinson (Baker, 1989), 71–80. https://www.preachingtoday.com/sermons/sermons/2005/august/0364.html

12 Donald R. Sunukjian, "The Cripple's Story," in *Effective First-Person Biblical Preaching*, J. Kent Edwards (Zondervan, 2005), 156–161.

13 Dean Jones, "Saint John in Exile," https://www.youtube.com/watch?v=SpdjmxTK_6g.

### Should I wear a costume?

As implied above: not necessarily. While I have seen costuming done well, most of the time it is not necessary, and sometimes it hinders the ministry. Listeners can be distracted by novelty or the embarrassment of a bathrobe drama if it is not done at a high standard. My rule of thumb: "less is more." Give people enough to spark imagination but not dominate attention.

The rule of thumb can edge toward the right if the narrator wears something simple such as a jacket or scarf. Likewise, the preacher-as-storyteller might use modern dress such as Zacchaeus in a business suit, or Joseph the carpenter with a tool belt.

### Should I use props?

In contrast to my hesitation about costumes, I am an advocate of props if they are simple—a pair of crutches (set aside for 95% of the story); a small, ornate box; or an oil lamp. These low-tech visuals help convey character and transport listeners to the ancient setting. When preaching on the revival under King Josiah (2 Chronicles 34), I used a third-person perspective with a twist. I brought volunteers to the stage who were the same age as Josiah as the story progresses: eight years old, then twenty, then twenty-six. Stage movement ("blocking") can also be a simple tool of visual communication. You might remove the pulpit and stand, sit, or walk around to help convey content and mood. This raises a corollary question: if I don't have a pulpit, where should I place my notes? The answer is easy. Don't use notes.

### Where is the speaker located in time?

Two options: take the audience back in time or bring the speaker forward. One of my students did the first. As Jonathan's armor bearer, he told the story of how he and the prince had taken on the Philistines (1 Sam 14). As the student began, he was seated, sharpening a blade with a whetting stone. (He must have gotten permission to bring a short sword into the classroom!) He "noticed" the listeners and invited them to join him around the campfire: "Wasn't that some battle today? What? You didn't hear about it? Well, let me tell you about my master, Jonathan." Then he set aside the blade and told the story.

John Reed's monologue also takes the audience back in time.[14] Abraham has just returned from Mount Moriah, and he recounts the harrowing story to Sarah. The audience overhears Abraham's faith-building account as if they have been invited into the tent.

In "The Broken Heart of David Jessison" mentioned above, Robinson uses the second option. He comes forward in time: "When I accepted the invitation to be here, I didn't realize that this was what you call 'Fathers' Day.' I don't have much to say about being a father…. . I can't give you much help for being a successful father."

In both options, as you beam in and out of time, be careful to avoid anachronisms. The audience can suspend their disbelief that somehow David knows about "Fathers' Day," but the ancient king should not have knowledge of antibiotics or Google. Neither should Abraham have knowledge of the Ten Commandments since they were not yet written.

### Should I read the text before telling the story?

You have freedom here. Some homileticians warn that reading the text destroys tension, but I have not found that to be true. Most people need to hear the text two or more times to grasp what is going on. If the text is long, as is often the case with narrative sermons, you might select key verses to read. You could do this in a traditional introduction, or perhaps a leader in the church might read the text before you expand it with the story.

The next strategy for expanding our creativity is similar to the first-person narrative but pushes right on the continuum.

---

14 John Reed, "Abraham's Return from Mount Moriah," in *Telling Stories to Touch the Heart: How to Use Stories to Communicate God's Truth*, by Reg Grant and John Reed (Victor, 1990), 89–93.

## Strategy 6.2: Try Drama

If members of your church have experience with theater, you can leverage their gifts by asking them to partner with you for a special occasion. You might read the passage and give a short homily before leaving the stage to the actors. By the way, enlisting dramatists in ministry will bless them because Christians in the arts often feel ancillary to the church.

In lieu of staging a full or partial drama, a daunting undertaking, you might stretch your own creativity. Haddon and Torrey Robinson did this with a modified drama. To present Matthew 2:1–18, one of the speakers interviewed Herod the Great, giving special attention to the slaughter of the innocents.[15] I also did this with Galatians 1, playing two parts. As I studied the text, I realized that we were overhearing one side of a debate. Paul was defending his apostleship and the gospel of grace against the "Judaizers." When my exegesis was done and I started to make decisions about the form of my sermon, I thought: "I could just explain the historical circumstances and theology of works-religion, or I could *show* them." I opted for showing, so I set up two lecterns on the stage and played both sides of the debate: "Resolved: Paul's gospel is man-made."

## Strategy 6.3: Try "Dramatization"

This is similar to 6.2, but does not mean staging a play; rather, the preacher shows the truth by depicting it verbally in a scene. The technique goes back to Cicero and Roman rhetoric. They called it *evidentia*: "A great impression is made [on an audience] by ... [an] almost visual presentation of events as if practically going on."[16] A few passages of *evidentia* can enliven a sermon or speech. I did this when I preached from Nehemiah 3. I was making the point that God is present in our work, even when it seems mundane such as hauling stones and winching them into place to rebuild the wall:

---

15  Robinson and Robinson, *It's All in How You Tell It*, 107–114.

16  Cicero, *On the Orator*, trans. H. Rackam, ed. Jeffrey Henderson (Harvard University Press, 1942), 161.

At the end of a long day, maybe one of the workers went home, and his wife said to him:

"What did you do today?"

"You know. I was working on the wall."

"Uh huh. How did it go?"

"Well, we placed four stones."

"That's it? The whole day? Just four stones?"

"Yep. For the longest time we couldn't find a stone that fit. Then the pulley broke, and we had to wait to borrow the one from the team next to us. And then there was lightening in the west—did you see it?—so the foreman told us to stand down until the rain passed. But it never did rain. We just stood around for a while. [pause] And we placed four stones."

God enabled that fellow to place those four stones. God is behind and before and under and over and through this story. Your story too. When you go to a board meeting, God is enabling you. When you chase a toddler, he is with you. When you do a pre-service microphone check, God is enabling you. It's hard for us to feel that way about our own work, isn't it? It's all so mundane. Or is it? We need Nehemiah to remind us that God is at work in us, to will and to do his good pleasure. God enables your work.

### Strategy 6.4: Try Parable

What an enchanting form: a fictional story that compares something earthly to something spiritual. When preaching from a narrative parable, you might modernize it. The farmer might use a cultivator, the king might be a prime minister, or the Pharisee might be a seminary professor. For even more creativity, you could create an original parable as a natural way to expound the biblical parable.

I have also seen parables called into service with non-narrative texts such as proverbs. Behind each proverb is a portfolio of "case studies" (stories) which the sage has reified into a pithy statement. So, you might create a fictional but realistic story to illustrate the proverb. That is what Sid Buzzel did with Proverbs 4:23, "Keep your heart with all vigilance, for from it flow the springs of life."

His narrative sermon is called, "The Story of Anna McLeash."[17] A Bible college student is hired by Mrs. McLeash to do yard work on her impressive estate, and that student narrates the story. She gives him more and more responsibility until one day she dismisses him because a new man—Tom—has come into her life. He is witty, charming, and handsome. Over the course of two years, he wheedles his way into her heart and her bank account, and by the end of the story she is bankrupt and homeless. Buzzel concludes with a pastoral word:

> The story I have told you is true, just as a parable is true. Anna and Tom didn't really exist, but they do. They are like thousands of people who try to be secure, but they have not secured their hearts. Don't give your heart to anyone or anything that is not absolutely trustworthy.... 'Above all else, guard your heart, for it is the wellspring of life.'"[18]

### Strategy 6.5: Try Testimony

If the preceding heights of creativity have made you dizzy, this one comes back to earth. Anna Carter Florence defines "testimony" as a non-fiction story "of events paired with a confession of belief."[19] A personal story of salvation, or of one's daily walk with God, is a subtle but powerful apologetic for the reality of the Faith. That is how Paul used his own testimony in the book of Acts (22:1–21; 26:1–23). Such "proof" is difficult to argue with, as it employs much of the rhetoric we have talked about in this book such as indirection, emotion, and concrete imagery.[20] As Austin Tucker states, "The truth enters the imagination and finds a home in the soul."[21]

---

17 Sid Buzzel, "The Story of Anna McLeash," in *It's All in How You Tell It*, by Robinson and Robinson (Baker, 2003), 99–105.

18 Ibid., 105.

19 Anna Carter Florence, *Preaching as Testimony* (WJK, 2007), xiii.

20 Andrew Gurevich and Jeffrey Arthurs, "Theological and Rhetorical Perspectives on Self-Disclosure in Preaching," *Bibliotheca Sacra* 157/626 (April–June 2000): 215–26.

21 Austin B. Tucker, *The Preacher as Storyteller: The Power of Narrative in the Pulpit* (B&H, 2008), 58.

To illustrate a biblical story or truth, we might enlist a member of the church to share his or her experience. Pastor Rick Warren has done this for many years. We might also use testimonies from history such as the conversion of Chuck Colson as recounted in *Born Again*.[22] To illustrate Romans 5:20–21, Buttry presents a monologue as John Newton, and Michael Gourlay uses the story of Archbishop Cranmer to illustrate Mark 8:34b–35.[23]

Strategy 6—Expand Your Creativity—should keep us busy for the next Sunday or two. The appendices take us on a guided tour of two sample sermons to see what the principles of this book look like in complete messages.

## For Further Study

- Arthurs, Jeffrey D. *Preaching with Variety: How to Re-Create the Dynamics of Biblical Genres*. Kregel, 2007.
- Lewis, Ralph L., and Gregg Lewis. *Learning to Preach Like Jesus*. Crossway, 1989.
- Robinson, Haddon W., and Patricia Batten, eds. *Models for Biblical Preaching: Expository Sermons from the Old Testament*. Baker, 2014.
- Tucker, Austin B. *The Preacher as Storyteller: The Power of Narrative in the Pulpit*. B&H, 2008.

### Talk about It

- What are the strengths and weaknesses of the first-person form?
- Do you have people in your congregation that would enjoy partnering with you to preach with creativity—drama, visuals, research, dialogues, etc.? How could you find out what resources you have?

---

22 Charles W. Colson, *Born Again* (Chosen, 1976).

23 Buttry, *First-Person Preaching*, 105–111; Michael Gourlay, "Thomas Cranmer, 1489–1556: Archbishop of Canterbury, Martyr and Liturgist," in *Please! No More Boring Sermons*, ed. Keith Weller (Acorn, 2007), 167–176.

## Dig Deeper

This book is about preaching historical narrative, but how could you take the same approach with other genres? That is, what are the literary features of proverbs, parables, poetry, etc., and how could you reproduce their effects in your sermons? Start with parables since many of them are narratives. What happens when we listen to a parable? How can you do the same thing when you preach from a parable?

## Practice

One of the sample sermons in the appendices is about Zacchaeus (Luke 19:1–10). It is third-person. Sketch in a few bullet points how the sermon would be different if preached from Zacchaeus's perspective. Do the same for another first-person perspective, perhaps a person in the crowd.

# Conclusion

Once upon a time, a preacher traveled far and wide with messages about Jesus and his word.[1] The people loved to hear him, and crowds gathered when he came to town. This led other ministers to ask him the secret of his success. He told them that he simply tried to make things accessible to the people in the pews. In particular, he recommended story. He said, "There's no better way to make doctrine and ethics clear, interesting, and potent. Narrative is powerful rhetoric, and it's the primary way that God has given us his word."

The ministers gave him a skeptical look: "Sir, it seems to us that you are not being fair to your own gifts with all this emphasis on story. Some of us went to seminary with you, and we have seen your gifting and the depth of your learning. Why do you emphasize story when it seems that you should just emphasize truth. Why don't you just present truth as truth?" The traveling preacher thought for a moment, and then said:

> Once upon a time Truth came to town. He looked intimidating because of his bulging muscles and stern countenance. Some people remembered when Truth had confused them, and some remembered when he had hurt them. So, most of the

---

1 This story is an adaptation of a rabbinic parable. Many versions exist including https://petercorney.com/2012/04/01/truth-and-the-power-of-stories. The version I follow most closely in my own retelling is from Bryan Chapell, *Using Illustrations to Preach with Power* (Zondervan, 1993), 187–189.

townspeople stayed out of the street when Truth came to town. Only the strongest of the people spoke with Truth.

The next day Story came to town. He looked like the townspeople and dressed in ordinary clothes, but he told them of all the places he had been and the sights he had seen. The people loved Story's visits. They came out of their houses to greet him and then invited him in for coffee and pie.

Truth watched all of this and was confused and embarrassed. Then he became angry, blaming the townspeople for being shallow and weak. Story saw him sitting alone in the park and asked him about his troubles. Truth blurted out, "I am the truth! They should listen to me. I mean them no harm. I can help them."

Story thought for a moment but said nothing. Instead, he took off his hat and coat and put them on Truth. Truth was transformed. He was still powerful and well-educated, but now the people saw him in a new light. They invited him into their homes and listened to his counsel. They laughed and cried with him. After he departed, they thought often about his stories, and talked among themselves about what he had taught them.

To this day, when Truth goes to town, he puts on Story's clothes so that people will consider his wisdom and come back for more.

## Third-Person Narrative Sample Sermon
## "Zacchaeus" (Luke 19:1-10)

*Jeffrey D. Arthurs*

### Background

THE STORY BEGINS near the end of the story; that is, it takes place near the end of Jesus's life on earth. The story takes place about four days before he enters Jerusalem—we call it the "Triumphal Entry"—and about ten days before he is crucified—we call it "Good Friday." He is walking to Jerusalem, his eyes forward and his face set like flint. But he's not in Jerusalem yet. He's on the road to Jerusalem, and to reach the Holy City, you have to pass through Jericho.

> The sermon does not use a traditional introduction. It plunges straight into the story. As you will see, the background is unusually long, but the cultural and geographical information I share is important to the story. I try to make the background interesting with concrete language and point of view. That is, I describe Jericho as if the camera were wandering over the region.

*Verse 1: He entered Jericho and was passing through.*

It's a beautiful time of year—Spring—already warm down there in the Jordan valley. They called it the City of Palms, a kind of Palm Springs for wealthy people so they could escape the damp winters in Jerusalem. Herod has his winter palace there. It has reflecting pools, a grand staircase that overlooks gardens, and fifty niches in the walls for statues. He also built a theater there and a hippodrome for racing horses. And Jesus is passing through.

It's a rich city, located at the intersection of the major north-south road and the major east-west road that leads up to Jerusalem. As you walk through Jericho, you might notice groves of balsam trees that have made the city rich. Balm comes from balsam trees, an aromatic resin used in medicines and perfumes. The ancient historian, Josephus, said that balm is the "most precious thing there is." And Jesus is passing through.

But I don't think he gazed in awe at the palace, or inhaled the fragrance of the balm, or cocked his ear to catch the sounds of the races in the hippodrome, because when a man has heard himself sentenced to death, he loses interest in carnivals. But he didn't lose interest in people.

### Verse 2: And there was a man named Zacchaeus.

> Notice the style of the language here and throughout. It is both vivid and oral. Designed for the ear, it uses direct address, short sentences, contractions, exclamations, fragments, etc.

That's a nice name, isn't it? It means "righteous one." So, here's a story about a good man, a good Jew. But not so fast. Keep reading:

### Verse 3: He was a chief tax collector and was rich.

"Righteous one" is a "chief tax collector"? Oh my! I hope you catch the irony. You might as well call the town drunk, "Sobriety," or the town prostitute, "Chastity." You

> Exegetical material—the culture of tax collecting. I try to keep the material brief and mix it with modern analogies in the next paragraph ("Nazis," "Benedict Arnold").

see, the Romans had a system called "tax farming." They would subcontract the job of chief tax collector to the highest bidder. They would farm it out to whoever promised to collect this greatest amount of taxes. Anything collected above that sum was pure profit for the chief tax collector. So, he could gouge his fellow-Jews, or take bribes, or cheat, and Rome would turn a blind eye. The main collection centers of Roman-occupied Israel were Caesarea, Capernaum, and Jericho; so, if you were the chief tax collector in the City of Palms, you were indeed, as Luke says, "rich." "Righteous one" was a "chief tax collector." That's good!

But riches came at a price. Zacchaeus was a collaborator. He was in league with Rome. If he had lived in Holland during WWII, he would have sold information to the Nazis and ratted on his fellow countrymen. Maybe we should call him Benedict Arnold, or Judas. Furthermore, he was unclean. He worked with Gentiles; he handled their money; he probably worked on the Sabbath (the Romans didn't care about that holy day).

So, Zacchaeus is probably snubbed and excluded from the Jewish community. They call him names, send him hate mail, and pray against him. Of course, they never do this to his face. To his face they bow, tell him how fine he looks, and open doors for him. But he's seen their gestures when they think he's not looking. He's seen their sneers turn to plastic smiles as he approaches. Yes, Zacchaeus's wealth came with a price. Well, what does he care? He knows how to get even. He's laughing all the way to the bank.

> I use imagination and vivid language to *show* how Zacchaeus would have been an outcast. Also notice also how the sermon weaves Zacchaeus's inner monologue into the story. The audience overhears his thoughts and emotions.

We're a bit surprised, then, that the next statement in the story is:

## Conflict

**Verse 3: He was seeking to see who Jesus was.**

He wants to see Jesus? Well, now that I think of it, maybe this isn't so surprising. After all, everyone wants to see him. Jesus is at the height of his popularity. All the land has heard about the rabbi from Galilee. Some people said that he had power to heal, and just a few miles from here that fellow named … what was his name?

> Finally—the conflict! The background has hinted at conflict—Zacchaeus as a traitor and outcast—but here we finally arrive at a direct statement. However, the conflict lacks the power of physical action like David and Goliath. The conflict is psychological, within Zacchaeus, as he seeks Jesus. I try to depict the conflict in a way that builds from simple curiosity to desperation.

Lazarus? Yes, Lazarus from Bethany—oh my! Could it be true? Could this rabbi raise the dead? Some people were saying that he would deliver the Land. Zacchaeus wasn't sure he wanted the Land to be delivered. In any case, Zacchaeus was seeking to see Jesus.

## Rising Action

> The stair steps begin as the conflict intensifies. We see the action through Zacchaeus's point of view. First, his curiosity rises; then he becomes aware of his guilt and loneliness; then he becomes desperate as the crowd blocks his view; then he throws dignity aside, runs, and climbs a tree (but not without a struggle first); then Jesus accepts him, then the crowd opposes this act of kindness.

But what a crowd! Thousands and tens of thousands of pilgrims are walking to Jerusalem for Passover. The citizens of Jericho have come into the streets to bless the pilgrims—that was their tradition. As the procession slowly snakes through Jericho, Zacchaeus is scanning the pilgrims. Which one is Jesus? Someone starts to sing a psalm of ascent, and other people join in. Dust is rising. Which one is Jesus? Zacchaeus hears someone on his right say something about the beggar who sits just outside the gate of the city—something about a healing. Zacchaeus hears someone on his left utter the word "messiah." People are standing on tiptoe, craning their necks. Women are lifting their babies, asking for a blessing. Everyone wants to see Jesus. Zacchaeus wants to see him.

This is more than curiosity, more than interest in the latest celebrity. Zacchaeus wants to see Jesus because, well, he isn't sure; but he feels driven. His heart is restless. Today we would call him a "seeker." Maybe Zacchaeus had come to that place in life where his robes, and rings, and chains of gold have lost their appeal. Zacchaeus may be on top of his game—the game of making money—but it no longer seems to be a game worth playing. He owns a villa with a marble fountain in the courtyard. So what? People call him sir, and he has a staff of tax collectors and bookkeepers, but he's still restless inside. He's often invited to the Romans' banquets, but this matters less to him than it used to. When he looks at himself in the bronze mirror in his villa, what does he see? A man of the world: the finest robes, a confident look, but tight lips, and a pugnacious tilt of the chin. And if the mirror could reveal what is inside, he would see a troubled heart. He is not an honorable man. He's lonely. He wants to see Jesus.

He's heard that Jesus accepts sinners. They call him the "friend of sinners." Why, he's heard that a tax gatherer travels with Jesus. So, Zacchaeus is trying to see Jesus.

But he can't. He's too short! Zacchaeus was a wee little man, and he can't see over the crowd. The sound of the pilgrims is coming closer. A tambourine is tapping the rhythm. What are they singing? Psalm 121? "I will

> The quick allusion to the Sunday school song adds a light touch. If people do not know the song, nothing is lost.

lift up my eyes to the hills." Zacchaeus is bouncing on tiptoes trying to see Jesus. He's grabbing shoulders to bounce higher, but it's no good. He can't see over the crowd. He walks ahead to find a vantage point, but it's no good. The crowd is traveling with the pilgrims. He can't see. So, he pulls up his robes, throws dignity aside, and runs. Yes, you heard me correctly: Zacchaeus, the chief tax collector, runs. Running is for boys, not men of authority, but he runs.

### Verse 4: So he ran on ahead.

What's this? A tree. A sycamore fig tree with a low trunk and broad branches. He could climb it. But, his dignity! Men don't climb trees! That's for boys. But the procession is coming. He eyes the tree—yes, if he stretches he could grab that branch, he could put his foot there. Here comes the crowd. It's now or never. Dignity be hanged, and up he goes.

> Remember the power of delivery. Here and throughout I use voice and body to convey point of view, especially Zacchaeus's emotions. Gestures, facial expression, and vocal variety are missing from the printed page, so try reading the manuscript aloud. Read with imagination. Remember that the listeners will match your emotional state when conveyed through the nonverbal channel—the power of empathy.

And here comes Jesus! Zacchaeus thinks: "I suppose that's Jesus. The others seem to be following him and protecting him from the crowd. His eyes are down. His thoughts seem elsewhere. He seems out of step with the parade. I wish I could talk to him."

*Verse 5: And when Jesus came to the place, he looked up.*

Their eyes meet. The crowd accordions and bumps into each other. Jesus says, "Zacchaeus." The noise of the crowd dies down. The sound of a flute fades away. The crowd heard the name, "Zacchaeus." They all knew Zacchaeus. What about Zacchaeus? And what's Jesus looking at? Wait a minute! That's Zacchaeus! In

> You may have noticed that I simply retell the story verse by verse, like a stereotypical expository sermon. But I'm doing so with sensitivity to genre. The only section I do not read word for word is verse six, but I closely paraphrase that verse in my own narration.

the tree! A boy points and laughs, but his father shushes him. What is Jesus saying?

*Verse 5: "Zacchaeus, hurry and come down, for I must stay at your house today."*

Zacchaeus thinks: "Come down? Yes, of course." There is a tumble and a rush; a branch snaps; his robes balloon out; and then Zacchaeus is down, standing before Jesus, no he is *bowing* before Jesus. He takes him by the arm, welcomes him joyfully, and leads him home.

*Verse 7: And when [the crowd] saw it, they all grumbled: "He has gone in to be the guest of a man who is a sinner."*

> Once again, remember the power of delivery. Convey verse seven with disgust and the listeners will collaborate with you to conclude: "That's wrong! The crowd shouldn't grumble at the kindness of Jesus!"

Doesn't it make you sick when Jesus is kind to sinners? It makes the crowd sick. The crowd likes it when Jesus does miracles, but they don't like it when he does mercy. He is offering a graduate school education in grace. Zacchaeus sits in the front row, but

the crowd won't even enroll.

They don't understand: Jesus came to do this. **He came to seek and save the lost.** He is now journeying in the high country to find the sheep that has strayed. He is now sweeping the floor to find the coin that was lost. He is now scanning the horizon, watching for the return of the prodigal. **This is his mission. This is why he came—to seek people like Zacchaeus, and to save them.**

> The third-person form is very flexible. Here I insert a brief analogy (graduate school). Just keep material like this brief. Keep driving the plot.

> I've placed the big idea in bold font to help you spot it. Notice how I repeat and paraphrase it.

Zacchaeus is so excited! Jesus is coming to his house! They're going to sit at the table together. For the first time in a long time, Zacchaeus feels accepted. Kindness rolls over him like a river.

> O the deep, deep love of Jesus,
> vast, unmeasured, boundless, free;
> rolling like a mighty ocean
> in its fullness over me.

> Quick support material (a line from a hymn). Once again, if people do not catch the allusion, nothing is lost.

**That's why Jesus came—in kindness to seek and save the lost.**

## Climax

*Verse 8: And Zacchaeus stood and said to the Lord (this implies that he "took his stance," he's going to make a speech; even though he addresses Jesus, he's also aware that the crowd overhears him): "Behold, Lord, the half of my goods I give to the poor. And if I have defrauded anyone of anything, I restore it fourfold."*

Are you hearing this? "Half of my goods I give to the poor"! That's a lot of goods! "And if I have defrauded anyone"—well, he knows that he *has* defrauded people. The construction of this Greek sentence is called a "first class conditional." This sentence is constructed as a conditional "if-then," but it could just as easily be translated here "*since* I have defrauded." There's no doubt about it. He *has* defrauded people. It might have been legal, but it was still sin. The Romans might have allowed it, but it was still sin. He has not loved God and his neighbor as himself. "And if I have defrauded anyone of anything, I restore it fourfold."

Do you know what we're seeing? Repentance. **We are seeing the kindness of Jesus lead a sinner home.** We misuse our neighbor, and look out for number one, and rationalize our meanness, and try to hide our emptiness under a mound of things; but when Jesus looks at you, and calls your name, and invites himself to your house, and accepts you despite the crowd, then we recognize that all our flimsy excuses for bad behavior are just flimsy excuses. **Jesus came in kindness to lead people to repentance.**

> My language becomes more direct, using the first and second person ("Are you hearing this?" "Do you know what we're seeing?" "We misuse our neighbor.") Hopefully, the listeners have identified with Zacchaeus in his success, loneliness, conviction over sin, and desire to see Jesus. In the last paragraph, I set the story aside and speak pastorally to the congregation: "Have you met Jesus?"

## Resolution

*Verses 9–10: And Jesus said to him, "Today salvation has come to this house, since he also is a son of Abraham. For the Son of Man came to seek and to save the lost."*

> The sermon ends with brief, direct exhortation. I usually draw out the application with a few paragraphs, but this sermon ends quickly after the resolution of the story. If you wanted to apply this story to believers rather than unbelievers, you could conclude by talking about Jesus's compassion for the lost and his courage to fulfill his mission despite the crowd, and that we should follow in his steps.

Have you met Jesus? If you haven't, why not today? You might say to him: "Lord, I'm a sinner. I've looked out for number one, I've done wrong, and I've alienated myself from the community. You know. But you are still seeking me. You are calling my name. Lord, please clean me up, inside and out. Please save me. Amen."

# Appendix 2

## First-Person Narrative Sample Sermon
## "The Broken Heart of David Jessison" (2 Sam 13-18)

### *Haddon W. Robinson*

The introduction seemed a little strange this morning. I am seldom introduced as David Jessison. Most folks know me simply as David. No one calls me Dave. I have been looking forward to this opportunity to speak to you. But when I accepted the invitation to be here, I didn't realize that this would be what you call "Father's Day." I don't have much to say about being a father. I would have been better prepared to speak on Veteran's Day or even President's Day. I can't give you much help on being a successful father. I say that with both embarrassment and grief.

> Robinson provides a brief introduction in character, speaking as David. He helps the listeners grasp what is happening (a first-person story) without stating baldly: "I am telling a story from the perspective of . . ." He also orients them to the topic—David's failure as a father.

You see, I have been a success in almost everything I did. I made my mark in the military. In fact, when I was just a teenager I enlisted in the Israeli army and helped to win a strategic battle against our enemy the Philistines. Throughout my younger years, I won significant battles. We were overmatched and undermanned, sometimes by twenty to one. I must say that I rather enjoyed those battles, guerilla

> To create identification with his target audience, fathers, the preacher first describes his accomplishments. These accomplishments then act as a foil to David's failure as a father. Robinson does not say so, but he is implying that we can gain the whole world but lose the souls of our children.

warfare. Later I commanded an army of over 250,000 soldiers. I think it is fair to say that because of my leadership, Israel became the most dominant nation in western Asia.

But I wasn't simply a general. I also had to be a statesman. I molded Israel into a nation and elevated it to its greatest power. When I came to the throne, the nation was brick. When I left, it was marble. I think my predecessor, Saul, did as well as he could, but frankly, when he was killed, the country was near chaos. But after my forty years as king, Israel was in her glory. For example, I

> Robinson was a master of language, slipping metaphors into the story like this one: "the nation was brick, but I left it marble." Later he will summarize Absalom's protracted plotting of revenge: "He sucked that lemon for two years."

instituted law courts, developed commerce with surrounding nations, appointed a superintendent of agriculture, and contributed to the arts. I organized the Levites and singers in the tabernacle. I know that this sounds like boasting, but let me simply point out that historians have described my era as the "golden age of Israel."

But if you really want to get to know me, you have to know what I was on the inside. Believe it or not, I have the soul of a poet. I have been a singer and musician. As a lad I learned to play the rubaba, a crude instrument with only one or two strings. That instrument could not hold the music of my heart. Later in life, I invented more elaborate instruments. My music captured the many colors of life. You know some of the songs I have composed. You have them there in that book. No, not the hymnbook. The Bible. I wrote at least seventy-three of what you call the "psalms." Those hymns express the whole range of human emotions. Some are alive with joy. Others express my struggles and doubts. Some I wrote only for myself. I never thought that they would be published.

What I am trying to say is that most people in my time and since have considered me a brilliant success. Some people write history, and others read it, but I made it. That's what God enabled me to do. Yet, what I must confess to you this morning is that I was a failure as a father.

I don't want to bore you with family history, but perhaps it could be some help to you. At a critical period of my life, I had an affair. It didn't seem like much when it began, but it escalated and got out of hand. I tried to cover it up, and that led to deceit and murder. Even though God forgave me for what I did, the whole thing had a dreadful effect on my family.

> A narrative sermon does not announce propositional points, but it still uses transitions that lead the listeners from one scene or idea to the next ("Yet, what I must confess is that I was a failure as a father.")

One of my sons, Amnon, forced himself upon his half-sister, Tamar. After he raped her, he pushed her out of his life like garbage. Incest and rejection devastated her. Her full brother, Absalom, came to hate Amnon, and he determined to avenge her. I don't need to go into the whole story, but for two years he sucked that lemon. He threw a feast at harvest time and murdered Amnon. Maybe that wouldn't have happened if I had acted myself to punish Amnon. But after my own sin, I found it very, very difficult to rebuke my sons.

Absalom rebelled against me. He determined to steal my throne, and he had what it took to do it. He was a handsome man, strikingly handsome, with flowing, long hair—the envy of men and the attraction of women. He was charmer. Believe it or not, but he stole the hearts of the people overnight. He promised them anything they wanted. He flattered them. He had uncanny ability—one of those men born to be king.

> Remember that the first-person perspective gives unrivaled opportunity to show the inner world of the narrator. Here, David reveals his attitude toward Absalom: "he was a charmer, born to be king." That permissive attitude was even more evident when Robinson delivered the sermon live. He smiled and chuckled at his "charming" son.

He got so many people to follow him that I had to leave the city with my army. But Absalom would not rest until I was destroyed and out of his way. We were headed to battle, and everyone knew that however the battle went, I could not win. You see, if Absalom lost, he would be slain or taken captive in disgrace. But if he defeated my forces, then I would be dethroned and probably killed. So, either way—win or lose—I would lose.

My associates did not share my high opinion of Absalom. They saw him as a traitor, and I'm sure they felt that he was the spoiled darling of an aging king. They wouldn't let me go into battle. They said something about my being too valuable. Well . . . I also suspect that they felt I was too old. Perhaps my generals suspected my stability. They knew how much I loved Absalom.

> What a character says ("Do not touch the young man") reveals inner motivation and thoughts. Quoting dialogue is a simple and efficient technique of *showing*.

So, they went off to battle and left me behind. The last words I uttered as my men departed were: "Deal gently with the young man," and "Beware that no one touch the young man, Absalom."

I understand that they divided the army into three groups, and the fighting took place in the forest of Ephraim. During the battle a tragic accident took place. My son Absalom was riding through a thick stand of trees, and his head caught in the branches of one of those trees. His mule went out from under him, and he hung there suspended between heaven and earth. He was helpless. I was told later that one of my generals found him there and put three shafts through his heart. He might as well have driven them through my heart too.

> Handling the time element of a story can be tricky when the narrator is not present when events occur. Here Robinson needs to be omniscient for a moment, stating that Absalom has died, even though David was not present at that event. The preacher-storyteller handles time seamlessly and most listeners would not even notice the shifts in perspective.

Of course, I didn't know what happened at the time. I waited for news. Two messengers came with communiqués. The first told me that my troops had performed valiantly and had won the day. I said, "Yes, but is it well with the young man, Absalom?" He avoided my question. Maybe he was too polite, or maybe he was afraid, or maybe he just didn't know.

Then the second messenger, a Cushite, came. He told me that the battle was won. "But what about the young man Absalom?" He responded, "May all the enemies of the king be like that young man."

And then I knew. I was devastated. The victory meant nothing to me. I went up to a room over the gates and sobbed, "O my son,

Absalom, my son, my son, Absalom. Would that I had died instead of you, O Absalom, my son, my son." I couldn't stop weeping. I had lost my son.

> These lines of lament are one of the emotional peaks in the literature of the Old Testament, or perhaps one of the deepest valleys. They must be delivered with sincere pathos.

I know what some of you are thinking: "Old man, your grief came too late. Don't come to us for pity." I haven't come for pity. I don't need your pity. But maybe you can learn from me. Feast on my carcass.

One thing I came to realize is that a child needs our personal influence. I should have known that. The most important passage in the sacred Law of God declared, "Hear, O Israel: the Lord our God, the Lord is one. Love the Lord your God with heart and with all your soul and all your strength. These commandments are to be on your hearts. Impress them on your children. Talk about them when you sit at home, and when you walk along the road, when you lie down, and when you get up." How can you

> The story is over. It is a tragedy. Robinson will now offer two applications: children need their father's time and their father's example. Unusually, the preacher makes these points while still in character. David "preaches" for a few moments. In my opinion, this does not feel contrived. What is your opinion?

do that unless you are with them? You need to take advantage of those special moments when nothing is happening and everything is happening.

Quite honestly, when Absalom was growing up, I didn't take much time with him. You see, I had a complicated family situation. I had seven wives and many concubines. I know that the Law speaks against that, but that's what kings did in my time. It was a way to establish alliances. It was part of the surrounding culture. I ended up with twenty children, and I was responsible for all of them. It was an impossible situation! No matter how much I loved my son, Absalom, I could only give him a tiny slice of my time.

That's not all. I was busy. I was busy with important matters. I had an army to direct, treaties to negotiate, and a government to organize. Given my schedule, I couldn't take time for a growing

> A simple transition: "That's not all." Robinson has not stated bluntly, "Point two," but that is what he is doing in essence.

boy, so I gave the responsibility to others. I suppose I wasn't in charge of my schedule, but it was in charge of me. One thing's for sure: when Absalom was a boy he never came to me with a broken toy; and when he was a man, he never came to me with a broken heart.

Look, permit me to tell you something. Time is not your friend. Time is your enemy. I know that it seems like family is as old as creation. Before there were nations, there were families. But *your* family, *your* family is fleeting. That's hard to feel. Seems like the children with always be with you. After all, they were with you yesterday and will be with you tomorrow, and it seems that they will be with you forever; but you only have them now, as they are right now. You cannot have your daughter at eight when she is twelve, and you cannot have your son at twelve when he is fifteen. No, time is not your friend. It is an enemy. It always works against us. If your major concern is your job, then time has won before you know it. Some opportunities will never return. Children need a father's time.

But that is not enough. Merely spending time with your children is not enough. A child also needs a father's example. I failed to provide that for Absalom. At a crucial time in my life, I let him down. I had an affair with Bathsheba. I spent a year or more in the far country. Absalom followed me. In his lovingkindness and according to his tender mercy, the Lord forgave me, and I returned to him. But Absalom didn't bother to return.

That passage in the Law that talks about spending time with your children also says something else. Something more basic. If you want your children to follow God, you have to follow him yourself: "These commandments will be upon *your* heart." I was going to tell you to be a good example, but forget that. Just be. Just be a sincere follower of God. Just be. Children pick it up.

I've rambled on long enough. I don't have much to tell you about being a good father. Maybe my experience can help you. Put first things first. Don't be a slave to your date book. Put some time in there for your children. I know how valuable your time is. You are providing for your family and building for the future, and you are to be commended for that, but if your time is so valuable, then shouldn't you give some of it to what is most valuable, your son or daughter?

That afternoon when I learned that Absalom had been killed was the worst day of my life. As successful as I was in my public life, I had failed my son. I went to my room and wept: "O my son, Absalom! My son, my son. Would that I had died instead of you, O Absalom, my son, my son." I meant that. I would have gladly died for him. But God had called me to live for him, and that was much more difficult.

> This dramatic monologue is not a Christ-centered sermon. It uses David as a moral exemplar—a negative exemplar. Most listeners find the sermon convicting, but some also find it desolating. After all, every father fails. If you added the good news of the gospel to this sermon, what would you say, and where would you place it? Would doing so rob the tragedy of its haunting power?

# Scripture Index

# Subject Index